Waiting for the REVOLUTION

A MONTANA MEMOIR

Waiting for the REVOLUTION

A MONTANA MEMOIR

Jo Anne Salisbury Troxel

Bozeman, Montana

ISBN: 978-1-59152-257-7

Library of Congress Cataloging-in-Publication Data on file.

Cover design concept by Allison Troxel

All images used are from the personal collection of
Jo Anne Salisbury Troxel except for the following:
Cover background photo from Canva photo
Wheat stem ornament revised from image at Freepik.com
Jean Jacques Henner's painting on page 119 used by permission of Bridgeman Images

Fore more information or to order extra copies of this book call
Farcountry Press toll-free at (800) 821-3874.

sweetgrassbooks
an imprint of Farcountry Press

Produced by Sweetgrass Books; Distributed by Farcountry Press
PO Box 5630, Helena, MT 59604; (800) 821-3874
www.sweetgrassbooks.com

Printed in the United States of America

24 23 22 21 20   1 2 3 4 5

For Rodney Russell Salisbury, my father (1887–1938),

R. Marie Chapman Hansen, my mother (1901–1976),

I dedicate this book, and thank them for my complicated, fabulous family.

Jo Anne Salisbury Troxel

FOREWORD

Sometime in the early 2000s, over a decade into my career as a geographer, I started studying local-level maps of Montana voting, particularly in presidential elections. I quickly noticed something unusual: One remote farming county in the far northeast of the state, Sheridan County, often voted much more Democratic than other eastern Montana counties, which have historically tended to vote more Republican. With some notable exceptions, this was true right up until 2012. Sheridan County voted for Adlai Stevenson twice, JFK, Hubert Humphrey, Jimmy Carter, and Bill Clinton (twice). The only one of these to win statewide was Bill Clinton in 1992 (narrowly). Sheridan County even very nearly voted for Barack Obama in 2008—only 34 votes separated him and John McCain.

As I dug deeper into the data it became clear that Sheridan County's Democratic lean was not limited to presidential elections. With some exceptions, Democratic senatorial, gubernatorial, and state legislative candidates often exceeded their statewide margins, whether they ultimately won or lost. So I asked myself why this might be the case. The most likely answer, I thought, had to do with demographics. Was this anomalous behavior associated with some kind of racial, ethnic, or religious difference? Surprisingly, the answer was no! Sheridan County is demographically almost identical to neighboring Daniels County—which is to say overwhelmingly white with a strong northern European, Lutheran influence but also other European national and religious influences (and very little else). Yet Daniels County has a long history of voting much more Republican than Sheridan County.

This meant that the answer likely had to do with something much more local and idiosyncratic. So I started investigating the history of Sheridan County. I discovered a series of volumes produced by the local historical society titled *Sheridan's Daybreak*. The first of these, published in 1970, included a brief history written by a local historian named Magnus Aasheim. Aasheim's history included several paragraphs about a group of politically radical farmers who came to dominate Sheridan County politics for most of the 1920s. These farmers' political movement included publication of a radical newspaper, *The Producers News*, which eventually became the official publication of the Communist Party USA's agricultural arm, the United Farmers League. In 1924 the radicals won a huge electoral victory, taking almost all countywide offices, including sheriff.

The story of the radicals' rise and fall in Sheridan County has been well documented by several other scholars. Suffice it to say that the radicals' political dominance was waning by the late 1920s and was largely defeated by 1932 (although Sheridan County still gave the Communist Party's presidential candidate its best showing of any county in Montana that year—a healthy 18 percent). But the link, if any, between Sheridan County's radical past and its more contemporary political leanings have not been explored.

In order to explore these links I felt it necessary to visit Sheridan County and track down descendants of both sides of the political drama that took place in the 1920s. I wanted especially to explore how the events of that time have informed the political consciousnesses, values, and ultimately voting behavior of these people, particularly those who have remained in Sheridan County. One of the people I found (though not in Sheridan County) was the last remaining child of the radical sheriff, Rodney Salisbury, and an equally fascinating woman named Marie Hansen. Rodney and Marie were both married to other people throughout most of the 1920s, and had three children together during this time (each also had several children with their spouses). The last living child of these three was Jo Anne Salisbury Troxel, the author of this memoir. Although she left Sheridan County as a child with her parents (who remained unmarried and were effectively exiled), she potentially had a great deal of knowledge about her parents, siblings, and others connected to Sheridan County that would be useful for my research.

Over the course of a two-day interview I conducted with Jo Anne in late 2009, the two of us bonded. Moreover I learned an enormous amount about Rodney, Marie, their relationship, their various children, and, most important, the impact of their politics and values on Jo Anne and her siblings (which was quite varied). Marie, in particular, has emerged as every bit as complex and important a figure as her more high-profile partner, Rodney. Indeed, the story of Rodney and Marie, as part of the larger drama of Sheridan County's radical past, has proven central to my understanding of Sheridan County as a place. And that is really the lesson, for me as a geographer, of my ongoing deep dive into Sheridan County's past and present: The stories of places are ultimately the stories of the people who make them—including, crucially, their relationships with the land. Readers will no doubt appreciate both aspects in this lovingly crafted memoir.

Larry Knopp, Professor Emeritus,
School of Interdisciplinary Arts & Sciences,
University of Washington, Tacoma

PREFACE AND ACKNOWLEDGMENTS

It never entered my mind that I would take on a project such as this memoir of my mother and father, and the Communist era of the 1920s and 1930s in Plentywood, Montana. But several things happened, and one day I put aside the novel I was writing, finished *Mean Dog Blues*, a poetry book, and sent it off to the publishers, and began this story. Now, four years later, this memoir of my parents is finished. Or maybe, more accurately, I should say I have abandoned it, finally. It has been a compelling, as well as interesting, journey.

Through the years, there has been the occasional phone call, and someone wanting to interview me about my father. Being the daughter of the Communist sheriff of Plentywood, I was of interest to students majoring in history, and a couple of times, I had been approached about doing a treatment for a possible movie, which seemed far fetched, and I declined. Happily, occasionally those calls were from people who remembered my father and mother and wanted to meet me. Several years ago, however, this interest became more academic. Larry Knopp, professor of geography from the University of Washington, and Gerald Zahavi, professor of history from the University of Albany, New York, came to interview me at different times, and from their different perspectives. They were both interested in Rodney Salisbury, the Communist era in Plentywood, but also in my mother, a married woman with two children with whom he had an affair. I was surprised at this shift. Most people interviewing me hardly mentioned my mother, Marie Chapman Hansen. Perhaps they thought I would be embarrassed if they did.

Through Larry and Gerry's interviews, I came to appreciate and understand much more about my own history as a descendant of radical parents from that small town in northeast Montana called Plentywood. I am grateful to both of them for making the history of my heritage come alive in a profound way, and for their interest in my mother, and giving her a face. I am happy to call them friends.

About this same time, a book titled *The Red Corner*, a scholarly work about Communism in Plentywood in the 1920s and 1930s, by Verlaine Stoner McDonald, hit the bookshelves. When I read this book, I recognized many names from my mother's memories and her elaborate stories. When McDonald mentioned my father and mother, I paused. They were a part of a complex time of social change, I understood, but they were more. Just as in my mother's stories, the struggle was not only with the harsh weather for farmers, but the differing ideologies of those farmers and the business element of small town Plentywood. My parents lived it.

My former colleague, Karen Waller, read the *The Red Corner*, and was impressed. "People need to know about the history of this part of Montana," she told me. "Since we are both from Plentywood, I think we should do a presentation for Pecha Kucha." Pecha Kucha is a popular community program, based on the Japanese business model, which limits presentations to 6 minutes, 40 seconds, with twenty slides. Bozeman's Ellen Theater hosts this event quarterly for ten presentations, and it is sold out both nights. Karen, much younger than I, growing up in the 1970s in that area, had heard of the turbulent Communist days of Plentywood in the 1920s and 1930s. We did the presentation in two parts: first, Karen presented the history as she heard it growing up in Plentywood; then I assumed the more personal role of my mother, explaining why she had had an affair with the Communist sheriff, Rodney Salisbury, and had three children with him, even though they were both married and had families with their spouses.

I thought that was the end of it. It had been a challenge, staying within the perimeters of the Pecha Kucha guidelines, but fun. Later, during the holidays, I was having coffee with Karen and our friend, Mary Beth Green, a great reader of history and especially biography. She slid a Christmas card toward me, and said "read it now." In it, she said I must write the story of my family, and she would help in any way she could. True to her promise, she has been with me in all the turns and twists of this endeavor and knows my family as well, if not better, than I do. To her, I am ever grateful. When Mary Beth was traveling, other editors helped me move it along. Karen DeCotis was a wonderful guiding voice, and got every nuance along the way. This is a much different script now, but she was the one who helped so much with her humor, her questions, her encouragement. My old friend, Ursula Smith, also an editor for *The Red Corner* was indispensable. Her expertise and encouragement, as well as her suggestions, gave me a better grip on the difficult multifaceted time of the 1920s and 1930s.

Marcia Prather, a voracious and critical reader read the manuscript like a physician, which she is, and had suggestions, as well as encouragement. Joy LeClair, a savvy radio interviewer, approached me about reading this story, because she eventually wanted to interview me for KGVM, Gallatin Valley Community Radio. She offered both positive insights and valuable suggestions. Pola Rest, erudite family friend, was an encouraging, helpful reader. I also want to thank the Plentywood librarian, Jonna Underwood, who was willing to do some much needed research in the archives of *The Producers News*, as well as the *Plentywood Herald*. She was ever gracious and helpful. I was also fortunate that my savvy neighbor, Valerie Dewey, would run from her house to mine, ready to help when I had a screaming computer problem.

Perry Frances and Tom Chaussee, whom I have known since we were children at Arlee, were in my thoughts as I wrote about life on the reservation. When we get together, the hills, valleys, and creeks return to us in all the magic of our youth.

I am thankful for all the voices that helped me articulate this memoir, especially the voice of my mother, R. Marie Chapman Hansen.

To my daughter, Allison Adaire Chapman Troxel, I thank her for her faith and encouragement, her willingness to help with techie problems, and her artistic treatment of the cover of this book. Marie, her grandmother, would have been proud of both of us.

HOW IT ALL BEGAN

It is a breezy day in Seattle with effervescent clouds, a lightness in the air. I love this town and come here often to visit a half-brother, Stanley Iverson. I am happy to be walking down Pine Street in an old summer dress and worn sandals to meet two women whom I have never met. I am fifty-seven years old and if my calculations are right, Jardis must be seventy-one, and Camilla, sixty-eight. They are my sisters.

These half-sisters felt old wounds: the breakup of their family, their father and my mother scandalizing the town by their affair. I stop in my tracks, realizing that all the participants of this time of turmoil know each other except my two brothers and me, who are new to the conflict. We are the "bastards," the illegitimate children of our father and mother.

As I get closer to the Bon Marche and the restaurant where we are to meet, I feel a flush of anxiety, my palms are sweaty. How will we know in the noontime throng of lunch seekers who we are? We have made no arrangements such as "I will be waving a red rose" or "I'll be the one with the black tam." We have done nothing to guarantee we will even find each other.

Outside the Bon Marche, I stop. There are so many stories about all of our families. I have lived my life in a vast and complicated narrative resulting in deep sorrows, sharp angers, melancholy minds. I think of my mother, her unconventional life, her drinking and losses, and her stories—always her stories. I see the image of my father, thoughtful with his high forehead and crisp-curly hair.

I take the elevator up to the fourth floor. I step through a door into a crowd of people. I stand there, uncertain, looking around. Two women get up from a bench and come toward me.

"We'd know you anywhere," one of them says.

Meeting my sisters now, all of us old women, I marvel at the passing of time and that after all these years it is actually happening. We are meeting;

we are talking. I had not even considered it a possibility, since the women in my father's first family were dedicated to hating my mother, accusing her of breaking up a marriage. They knew we existed, that we were related, but that was even more reason why they didn't acknowledge my two brothers and me as their half-siblings. We were a hateful abstraction in their minds—their father's children with my mother who had no right to exist.

It seemed impossible for people in the small Montana town of Plentywood to believe my mother and father, Marie Chapman Hansen and Rodney Salisbury, were totally dedicated to and loved one another. They were willing to give up their respectability, families, and careers to be together, and this was received with outrage and scorn. Perhaps (I know this is a romantic notion) they had a soul connection. Marie never fully recovered from his sudden death, the man she had three children with and loved for thirteen years. Various rumors circulated about Rodney's death, but the most pernicious one held that Marie poisoned him. Trying to trace the beginning of a rumor is like trying to catch the wind; it is passed along because it has an aura of intrigue and passion, and we humans thrive on such notions, even as we know they are probably false. Emma, Rodney's legal wife, knew the rumor, and entertained the idea with her family and friends; there has even been speculation that she may have started this rumor to get back at Marie, to tarnish her grieving. Anything they could do to malign my mother was justified. I always hold hope that my mother never heard this mean-spirited rumor. At any rate, it was not one of her stories.

I left that lunch, though, feeling an affinity for my half-sisters, Camilla and Jardis, my father's daughters with his wife, Emma. Our conversation naturally evolved into the politics of the day and we were in basic agreement. We discovered we were reading the same books, liked the same movies, shared revulsion toward war. Like our parents, we stood for unions and universal health coverage. Diplomacy was superior to war. As our conversation deepened we became animated and excited, appreciating each other's humor. "Well, I think we can agree, don't you, that Rodney and Marie were waiting for the revolution?" Camilla said. There was a storm of laughter. "What was the book Rodney said was the most important book of the twentieth century?" I queried. Without hesitating, we all shouted the answer in unison: *Ten Days That Shook the World*. Jardis asked, "Who was the Socialist running for president that Rodney voted for, and who spent time in jail?" Eugene V. Debs, an easy answer for us. With easy familiarity we talked about Tom Mooney, Big Bill Haywood, Upton Sinclair, Sinclair Lewis, Joe Hill, and the names of other radicals of the time. Then Jardis threw in a series of descriptions and we were to guess the name of the man: "He was an IWW. He worked as a migratory farm laborer, and he was from Bulgaria. He showed up in Plentywood in the spring." We mulled it over, and finally came up with Pete Steinov, and stories about him ensued. We had a wonderful time talking about how Pete visited each of our families, carrying gossip back and forth, giving and getting the latest news. This meeting was going better than any of us had anticipated. They told stories of our father and I was intrigued, having lost him when I was five years old. I felt their far-reaching sympathy, wanting finally to give me the father I had never known and to claim the sister they had never met. We were all reaching out to one another. I was both relieved and elated that this moment was happening.

Another tie we stumbled upon during our conversation was our common Latin teacher at Missoula Sentinel High School, Miss Wadell. She was Jardis's and Camilla's teacher when they first moved to Missoula in the 1930s, and my teacher in my sophomore year in the late 1940s. Miss Wadell had three outstanding dresses, and she rotated them on a weekly basis. We could describe them down to the last piece of lace, tuck, and pleat. She was a martinet for correctness and accuracy, and she dressed it every day. Her rigorous influence was one of the reasons Jardis became a Latin scholar.

I thought much about that encounter in the following weeks—how they knew me right away though I did not recognize them.

I was born into a life of intrigue and disruption. I was the femme fatale's daughter who resembled both her mother and our father in that way that genes pronounce themselves. All the principal players in the tragedy were long since dead, and nothing could be verified from them except through memories. "Here is my chance," I thought, "I can learn from Camilla and Jardis about my father. He will come alive for me beyond shadowy childhood memories. I will know why I am his daughter."

They knew my father, and I did not, aside from some images, as vague and indefinite as a child's drawing. They remembered my mother when she was young and lovely before worry, poverty, and drinking, along with being a social outcast, had humbled her into a worn woman at forty. I felt envious of them with their security as the legal children of Rodney. I wanted to be recognized as his daughter and their sister. Gradually, though, I began to see their side of the story: they were abandoned by their father for my mother. All they knew is that one day he was gone with Marie and their three children. They knew of his infidelity, placed the blame on my mother, and lived with that knowledge. But when he was gone, once and for all, with his lover Marie, they were stunned and angry. Our meeting, as the surviving women in both families was a healing toward understanding and acceptance. After our visit, I felt elated. What my sisters might make out of a hurtful and sad history could be revisited, made alive again, and perhaps retold. Maybe it could be rewritten and have a happier ending. Only once did the subject come up again, and that was a few months before Camilla died. Sitting across the table from me, she was back in time. She leaned toward me and asked, bitterly, "Why did your mother do it?"

"So I could be here for you in your old age, I guess." I reached across the table and took her hand.

Camilla assumed the role of my big sister. "I always wanted a little sister to boss around," she said. For the rest of her life, we were close. We went to Plentywood together and she showed me the town where I was conceived, and where she was born and lived as a girl. She told me endless stories of their life on the ranch in Plentywood, and what it was like being the radical Communist sheriff's kids. She had a prodigious memory, and many of her stories helped me frame this narrative. I met her three children—John, Nora, and Eugene Kelly—and though they were adults when I met them, they treated me like their aunt.

Unfortunately, I was never to see Jardis again. "It's too painful," she told Camilla. "There she was, so like her mother, small, animated, laughing, her expressions, her eyes, so like Rodney's. It took me back to that painful time in Plentywood." I was disappointed, because I had liked her so much, this Latin scholar who wanted to be a teacher. The story she told at that one meeting was important to me. Jardis had majored in Latin and graduated with honors from what was then Montana State University in Missoula. She was excited to be a high school Latin teacher. A position to teach Latin was open in a Montana school, and she eagerly applied for it. The superintendent had made inquiries to the principal in Plentywood and a minister in one of the Lutheran churches, and found out her father Rodney was a Communist. She never got the job, and never tried again. She was painfully aware that this information was more damaging than all of her stellar recommendations. The experience affirmed for her the injustice of those in power and resonated with all she had learned as the daughter of the Communist sheriff in Plentywood. For years, when I would question an injustice in the school where I taught, I would say to myself: "This is for you, Jardis." It made me feel better, because loving teaching as I did, I could understand her fierce disappointment in not fulfilling her dream.

I did hear from Jardis, though, one more time. I answered the phone late one night, and there she was, telling me about her open-heart surgery. I was so happy to hear from her, and she knew it and laughed. "I want you to know something, Jo Anne. I feel like you are my sister," she said.

I understood that for her, this was an important, generous act. One week later she died, and I mourned her passing, and that our acquaintance had been so brief.

Plentywood
Arlee
Missoula
Bozeman
Billings

1

Plentywood, Montana, circa 1900. In the very northeast corner of the state's map is a small town that my ancestors chose to be their entrance into Montana life. Montana had entered the Union in 1889, about twelve years before my family arrived in Plentywood at the turn of the century. With a name like Plentywood, I wonder if they had images of shade trees lining quaint roads with little forests and maybe even a friendly park. They would soon discover otherwise. The only wood in that landscape of gently rolling hills was the ponderosa pine along the banks of the Missouri and Yellowstone rivers. This is grass country, the land of pungent sagewort and bluebunch wheatgrass that nourished first the buffalo and antelope and later, cattle. The land here is prairie. The ancient glaciers that moved along this area left rich and fertile soil, good for grain production providing there is enough rainfall. It's a chancy place with long, below-zero, snowy winters and hot summers with capricious rain.

It's a town with one main street that ends abruptly at the Sheridan County Courthouse. The town of 400 people that my grandparents knew has grown out from main street, standing now with over 3,000 inhabitants, mostly farmers. The first business was established in 1900, and two years later, a United States post office appeared. It was on the map. As the county seat, Plentywood gets its share of business from the surrounding towns of Outlook, Scobey, Dagmar, Dooley, and Antelope.

My mother Marie's parents were Albert and Maggie Chapman, originally from Anderson, Missouri. They were in Joplin, Missouri, at one point, a place that experienced an economic boom in the late 1800s because of lead and zinc. The 1900 census shows the family in Illinois Township, Washington County, Illinois, where Albert listed his occupation as a well digger. Maggie's father, Saturna Bena, a doctor, had settled in Splitlog, Arkansas, where he practiced medicine and had a small gold mine east of town, but not much gold. Albert's father, Coleman, had been a Baptist minister, christening Maggie in the local river and officiating at their wedding. The family moved between Missouri and Arkansas, looking for work and hoping to find a place where they could raise their growing family: Cecil, Boice, Augustus, Coleman, Grace, and baby Marie.

They were small-town rural people who, with their parents, had witnessed the turmoil of Southern society during Reconstruction after the Civil War. Southern agrarian culture was trying to raise cotton without slaves, and the slaves were asking to be treated as free men, the assigned purpose of the war. The Ku Klux Klan became organized and took the matters of the African Americans into their own hands. No matter that the slaves were free by proclamation, the Confederate South kept the laws of segregation in place, and the KKK enforced the rules with lynchings, beatings, and threats to the blacks.

We know the stories of soldiers returning to ravaged towns, riddled with crime and the abandonment of a way of life. There was much work to be done to rebuild the country, but no money to do it. The Chapman family's decision to move west was a breath of hope in those times. By the turn of the century, they were ready to leave the South forever. People were ever moving westward with the promise of free land west of the Mississippi.

There was still some land to be homesteaded in northeast Montana, and the thought of the independence of free land and farming inspired the Chapmans. They worked and planned, saving for the day when they could make this move. They circled the spot on the map and marked the distance from Arkansas to Montana, traveling by wagon, boat, and train. The journey with six children going all those miles north almost to the Canadian border would be a challenge, but it was an adventure, too. The children, in the way of the young, thought it all very merry and exciting. My mother, Marie Chapman, was born in Rag Hollow, Arkansas, on January 1, 1901. The Chapman family came to this lonesome high plains country from Arkansas in the same year. She was seven months old. For her, she only knew Montana, and she always said she was born there.

When the Albert Chapman family arrived in Plentywood it was late summer. They stepped off the train into the hot wind of the high plains. It was too late to build a cabin, and the four boys, ranging in age from five to eleven, dug out the side of a hill for their winter refuge. They had arrived as a family of six children, and every two years thereafter another child was born: first Ann, then Eva, Jack, and Dick. There was always a baby in the house in those early Plentywood years, and one can imagine an exhausted and impatient Maggie. The four oldest boys were there to help, hauling water, washing diapers, gathering buffalo chips, tending the many chores of the ranch. There was little time for education, and survival depended on mindful, all-absorbing work, and even the youngest children were expected to do something to help.

They were pioneers, or maybe they were pilgrims in search of a spiritual renewal. But here they were, and here they would make a life. Albert worked for other farmers until he got a stake and land of his own the following October. He sold insurance, and Maggie, the doctor's daughter, midwifed the newborns throughout the territory. This desolate yet potentially fertile land was to be their home for the next twenty years.

This prairie country has a lonesome cast to the eye with its sweeping vistas, little springs and coolies, and the haunting two-noted cry of the mourning dove. All the towns here have a mythical attraction for me. The stories of my childhood were told in the lovely timbred voice of my mother. The first time I saw this country, I was in my early forties, many years after those pioneers had departed this mortal coil. It was high summer, and the acres of golden wheat undulated in the tireless sun. The shimmering gold of wheat in the last light of day with the eternal blue sky melting into the horizon left a lavender scrim across the landscape. One feels one's own insignificance in the face of the vast, indifferent space and longs for a voice, a companion, to bring one back. This country is sacred ground. My brothers Budson and Roger and I were conceived here, but we don't have experience of this land—only the memories that came from my mother's stories that influenced me all through my youth—stories of passion and betrayal, loss and disappointment. People loving each other and leaving, brothers fighting and dying.

2

There is a picture taken in a wheat field in Plentywood of Maggie and Albert with their children circa 1910. At the time of this photo they were well established in the community since their arrival nine years before. The photo is a record of better times for this family, marking an occasion. Maggie was going to take the train with her two youngest children back to Missouri to visit her parents and relatives. The newspaper photographer took this picture and featured it in the local newspaper, the *Plentywood Herald*. For years I kept this picture on the bookshelf in my study right above my desk. I had an endless fascination with it. I am related to all these people, my mother's brothers and sisters, but I know them mostly by the stories my mother told. In that picture I recognize something eternally true about that young girl, my mother.

Standing off to the side with a scowl is nine-year-old Marie. One can feel the energy in her willful little body, and the vulnerability, too. She wants more than anything to go on this train journey, but Maggie has decided: only the two youngest children are going.

The girl in that photograph, my mother, Marie, was a consummate storyteller, always transforming and shaping experience into a narrative. Her stories were intimate in feeling, an offering from her bewildered heart. There was so much loss and so little love in her young life, that she survived on memory culled through imagination. Her parents and nine brothers and sisters were characters in stories she told throughout my childhood about a way of life on a ranch in Plentywood.

So I lived on the prairie in my imagination through her stories. It seemed both an enchanted land and a haunted land. Circling these stories is a voice from my university anthropology professor, giving us the essence of Margaret Mead: "Culture shapes."

For my mother, this land shaped her inner landscape. It became an essential part of her character with its endless scope for the mind and dreams. She never tired of its volatile ways and harsh expressions. It fitted well her own dramatic and passionate personality. It was quite simply the land she loved all her life. I can hear her voice haunted by melancholy framing the experience, telling the story to herself, though I was the one who listened.

The wind was always blowing, always, and I would tie a scarf around my hair and button my coat and venture out to see . . . just to see what was there and there was always something for my curiosity to feed on. I wish I could explain to you how beautiful it was, the sky so big, the endless horizon, the way the sun dropped and then it was suddenly thick darkness. Sometimes you could see a dust storm developing miles away, just a swirling kaleidoscopic cloud in the distant sky, and then getting closer and closer and running for the house and battening down the windows, the doors, and listening to it howl around the corners, shake the house with its angry, wild cry. It was scary, but finally it would pass, wind lulled out of its fever. We would begin to clean the house, clear the islands of sculpted articulated sand in and around the house. The boys and papa would look to the cattle that stood mute like sand sculptures. So the dust storms gave fair warning but you had to care enough to watch and to understand what you saw.

I walked through the bunchgrass and the sage for miles just watching the skies, looking at the shapes and color of things, the red, pink, and yellow rocks. I once saw the biggest snake I have ever seen. It was coiled beside me. I almost stepped on it! Terrified, I ran all the way home. The boys just laughed and said it was nothing, but Papa wanted to know all about it. When I told him the size, its horrible nose and glittery eyes, he said it must have been a western hog-nosed snake. "I'm glad to see you're careful on those walks of yours," he said. "This land is full of dangerous snakes. Always take Fen with you."

In 1908, my grandfather, Albert Chapman, was appointed United States Land Commissioner by President Theodore Roosevelt. The next year Congress passed the Reformed Homestead Act that gave 360 acres to each claimant with the understanding it took more land in this rugged country to survive than in more moderate climates. Albert knew the land, the curves and sweep of it to the horizon. He knew the good luck, bad luck, and failures that the land exacted from the hard-working. As Albert was busy filing homesteads, selling insurance, being a notary public, he soon had two offices, one in Plentywood and one in Glasgow. The Chapman land expanded eventually to a thousand acres, and they raised wheat and Longhorn cattle. Plentywood was growing. People were migrating to the high plains from the East, the South, and Europe. The Great Northern Railroad advertised free land in the West, and boasted of its fertility, how one could raise anything. The Germans, Scandinavians—especially Norwegians and Danes—hustled into a new Eden, into salvation from poverty and want through hard work. Albert Chapman was busy filling out forms and finding land for eager farmers, but he always had time to interrupt his work and send a loving note to Maggie. Sometimes, when he was busier than usual, he would persuade Maggie to come with him to help out in the office. Often, after a busy day, he would stay in town at his office, too tired to come home, and ask Maggie to come to him. In one of his notes to her, typewritten and dated December 1908, he says, "I have concluded to stay over, and will inform you dear wife that I will be waiting for you, I will be waiting to see your dear face enter my doorway the face I love so very much, and do not disappoint me under any circumstances dear wife, for you know that life has a great many disappointments for me, without you causing just one of them." [*sic*] In another letter, he says, "I will tell you stories of true devotion and will play the part of a boy again if you will just come over so here goes, dear wife, and I will remain here until 7:30 waiting for you and if I do not see you by that time I will hang my head like one dejected and wend my way toward my home swearing every step I take." [*sic*]

Sometimes, Papa would come home, and Mama would be in one of her bad moods, angry, finding fault with everything. He would hold her while she cried, saying little endearing things like, "There, there, Maggie girl." He would coax her out of the house to take a walk, and finally, she would go. We'd watch them walk away, papa with his arm around mama's shoulder, leaning into her. Sometimes we wondered if he knew how mean she could be to us, especially we girls. Gracie, seeing them in one of these tender moments, might whisper to me, "Does this mean another baby?" and we'd cover our mouths, stifling our laughter.

Marie often went into town with her father, even on days of inclement weather, so she wouldn't miss school. She recited poems to him, and he would laugh and say in that Scottish brogue of his, "Aren't you my clever little lass, for sure." He could read music, had a beautiful tenor voice, and taught her songs of his ancestral homeland. On those bitter, sun-filled winter days on the prairie they sang together all the way to town. It kept up their spirits. They sang harmony to "Auld Lang Syne" beyond the traditional New Year's because her father liked it so much. "Ah, the Robby Burns, now there's a man of lonesome thought," he'd tell her. But it was the old folk song, "Loch Lomand," that was his favorite, and hers, too, throughout her life.

Loch Lomond
You'll take the high road,
And I'll take the low road
And I'll be in Scotland afore you.
Where me and my true love
Will never meet again.
On the bonnie bonnie banks of Loch Lomond

On her lunch hour, Marie would go to his office and get the nickel he left for her in an old cup on his desk. She would run to the store to get her favorite—an almond Hershey bar. When she returned, she would share it with him.

She often told me the story of how her dog, Fen, (after Fenimore Cooper), had gotten crazy and dangerous and her father had to shoot him. He explained to her that the dog was sick with rabies and was dangerous to everyone on the ranch. But she was inconsolable and uncharacteristically angry with her father.

Fen was a great dog, you know . . . walked the prairie with me when I was out looking for dried bones and kept the dangerous rattlers away. That dog was so full of joy . . . how he would run when he saw a prairie dog or a rabbit or a loitering bird. Just run and bark and yelp with joy. He slept on the bed between Grace and me, and he always knew when she was in pain from tuberculosis of the bone. He would lick my face, nudge my arm, so I would wake to her moaning, and tend to her. There were the nights, oh I will never forget those nights, with the wind howling and above it all, Grace's cry, a high keening of pain, and her leg stiff and hot, and the darkness which was filled with all this misery, the misery of a suffering universe. And Fen whimpering, wanting to help. I would rub her leg, give her sips of water, carefully wipe her feverish face with a cool towel while she cried, grabbed my hand, asking me over and over, "Am I going to die, Mariezi . . . or worse, be a cripple that people will mock and feel sorry for? I'd rather die!"

I didn't know how Grace and I were going to live without Fen; it was a serious thing for me, and Papa knew it. I was so angry, I didn't go to his office for weeks. Then one day, missing him, I ran to his office, and there was the cup, with nickels, a lot of nickels. He had put one in the cup every day. Oh, that was Papa. He knew so much, and he cared, like nobody else. And soon after that, when I arrived at his office for my nickel, there was a puppy! A brand new puppy, and Papa and I decided we'd name him Cooper and call him Coop.

She paused, thinking, and lit a cigarette. *But Mama, she didn't like it. Seems like she didn't like Papa to pay attention to me, sometimes I wonder if she even thought of me as her child.*

3

School in that bitter country was Marie's escape, her reprieve. It also put her at a safe distance from her mother, a demanding taskmaster, and the consuming needs of the household: the hauling water, finding buffalo chips for the fire, washing diapers, scrubbing floors, the ongoing preparation of food and endless dishes. Unlike her brothers and her sister Grace, she never missed school if she could help it. Her love of learning and her admiration for teachers and artists was rooted in this time. There was Prof Houston, from whom she learned the romantic poets and literature. They delighted her. On the ride to school in the horse and buggy, all bundled up to keep from freezing, she would jump out and run alongside the buggy to keep the circulation in her feet and recite poetry as she jogged along. On those cold, inhospitable days on the prairie, when the winds would usher in double-digit below-zero temperatures, she could recite by memory Wordsworth's "Intimations of Immortality" and her favorite, Coleridge's "Kublai Khan." She kept the rhythm of her walk in time with the poem. *In Xanadu did Kublai Khan / A stately Pleasure dome decree . . .* The time went by more quickly that way, and the play of her own mind transcended the misery of those harsh winter days. She spoke of Prof (a term of endearment) Houston so often, with such a starstruck tone, I knew he was the first love of her life.

He was the first person, besides Papa, to care about me, you know, the young, sad person I was, living in my fantasy world. He was my lucky star. He often quoted Rousseau to us in class, and it struck a chord in me. "The world of reality has its limits; the world of imagination is boundless."

It was clear, too, that she was special to him, this girl with her stories, her flamboyant wit. He was there for her, especially after the accident that almost ruined her life and looks.

Oh it was cold, those winters on the prairie. Sometimes the snow drifted so bad and the landscape was so changed in shape, that you could get lost in all that Moby Dick whiteness. Papa had a rope to the barn, and he and

Boice and Cec would follow the rope, staggering over mounds of drifts, try-
ing to see through the blizzard. When it would finally clear, we younger kids,
Jack, Ann, Eva, and sometimes Coleman, would get our sled and struggle to
this knoll about a mile away. We would slip under the barbed wire fence and
pull our sled up the gentle slope until we got to the top, and then we would
come roaring down, shrieking with terror and laughter. In the gloaming,
the sinking sun was leaving a streak of orange and pink like an elaborate
ribbon of rare silk in the evening sky. We trudged up the hill one more time
before it became seriously dark. Oh, you know how children are—so into the
fun and excitement of it all, you don't think of anything but the ride down,
getting slicker and faster all the time.

She paused here, lit a cigarette, leaned on the table, her head down.

We scrambled on that sled, and Colie gave us a push and then ran along
as we went faster and faster. I was sitting in the front, because Colie was
giving us the push and I was the biggest and the oldest. I was about fifteen.
There was that moment when I realized we were going so fast we couldn't
stop, and the barbed wire fence was there in front of us. We shrieked as we
ran into it, falling off, laughing as we rolled in the snow and the sled went
under the fence and finally stopped. Colie came running up, and when he
saw me, he said, "My god, Re . . . what did you do? There's blood . . . blood . . .
all over your face." I couldn't feel a thing, but then I could see the blood, a dark
shadow on the white snow. They took me into Plentywood, and the doctor,
I remember what he said, "This will take time, stitching layer by layer, so the
scar will not make an outrage of her face." That's what he said, imagine—"an
outrage."

While she was recovering, Prof Houston came to the ranch, bringing
her an eclectic assortment of books—*Wuthering Heights, Jane Eyre, The
Complete Works of Shakespeare, The Palmer Method of Handwriting,* and
Pilgrim's Progress. She continued her lessons at home so she could graduate on time. After supper, Prof Houston would read Keats and Byron to
her and Grace, both of them sitting up in bed wrapped in a blanket while
he sat close by with Coop asleep at his feet. They took turns reading "Ode
on a Grecian Urn" and Byron's "The Destruction of Sennacherib." Her
father often came and joined the group, and then they read Macbeth, be-

cause Prof said, "He had the right voice, that Scottish burr, an authentic touch." Grace played the part of Lady Macbeth so convincingly, with such dramatic flair, they had to pause and laugh when she said, "Screw your courage to the sticking point, and we'll not fail." That phrase became a family joke when times were especially hard.

Sometimes, while the girls dozed, Albert and Prof Houston would sing songs, talk about crops, the newest ideas about farming, what had happened to the Petersons, or the Schmidts, or the Lawsons, and why they had left the country discouraged, abandoning their homesteads. They formed a happy group: Grace, Marie, their father, and Prof Houston with his large laugh and funny stories. Then Maggie would come, scold the grown men for "exciting the sick girls, especially Gracie, with their wild goings on," and take the lamp, and they would follow her, apologetic, like a chidden train all the way down the stairs.

The wound healed and left a little indentation, like a dimple. With time, the scars were curious little flaws in a lovely face, dominated by large blue eyes with dark lashes. My mother was lucky. She was, my Uncle Colie said, "quite the looker." With age, that side of her face showed the scar intermingled with the wrinkles, and was hardly noticeable.

4

W hen I think of my mother's parents, it brings to life all the meaning of the Puritan work ethic. Their virtue could be measured in their ordinary, but necessary, life of great effort. Day by day existence for the Chapmans was defined by hard labor, and close behind it were civic responsibility and respectability. They soon became an established part of the community of Plentywood, well-liked and trusted citizens who paid their bills and kept their word.

Someone would show up needing a midwife, and Mama would put on her best dress, her gloves, her hat, and go back with them, looking stylish, but severe and sensible, and they trusted her. Once she was gone so long it was late the next day before she returned. It was a breech birth, and she had managed to save both the mother and child. Papa was so proud of her, and we all cooked supper for her, and celebrated.

My mother hesitated, turned and looked at me.

You know, that is one of the rare times I saw her happy, really happy . . .

Albert was known throughout the territory not only because he was United States Land Commissioner, but also because he was a Freemason—touted as the "oldest and largest fraternity in the world." During the fourteenth century, Freemasons regulated the stonemasons' qualifications. In those days, they used the three grades of the medieval craft guilds: apprentice, journeyman, and master. Masons have to believe in God, want to do good in the world, and be self-improving. In a small town such as Plentywood, the members attended Lodge to be around men they liked and respected. They had rituals, yet they were not a church. About certain rites they were pledged to deepest secrecy. They had a secret handshake, they said, in case you had trouble, needed help, or were in particular circumstances. Any man other than a Catholic could become a Mason, and the important leaders, businessmen, and ranchers of Sheridan County during the time the Chapmans lived there were members of this fraternal organization. In the hierarchy of that group,

Albert Chapman achieved the highest status, a 32-degree Mason.

Albert Chapman's Southern Baptist background made him a straight-laced, honest worker and teetotaler. It was a huge irony that the handsome Chapman boys had reputations as diligent workers, yet were also considered hard drinkers and wild daredevils. There were plenty of bars in the small surrounding towns to accommodate their need to break out of the repression of their straight-laced parents. According to my sister Camilla, respectable people found them scruffy, rambunctious, and brash. They were born to work and responsibility, school being a hit-and-miss affair for them. Maggie loved her boys, read to them, and taught them how to read, but the rigor, discipline, and consistency of regular formal education was sketchy at best. The ranch and making a go of it was the most important consideration. The Chapman boys knew how to repair machinery, break and shoe horses, pull calves, and ride herd on the Longhorns. In 1912, when Albert got his own brand, a tilted D touching the top of an A, the boys added branding to their skills. They were, in the best sense of the word, cowboys. Later, they would experience the handicap of their lack of formal education.

The two oldest boys, Cec and Boice, didn't always get along. Cec, because he was the oldest and Maggie's favorite, assumed the leadership of the ranch. Boice and he had different ideas about how the operation should be run, who should do what, who worked the hardest, and they often quarreled. Their disagreements ended in fights, curses, threats, and vows of lasting hatred. When they were in the throes of an argument, usually when they had been drinking, the younger children, especially Marie, disappeared, but typical of the Chapmans and their volatile ways, the boys would soon make up and, begrudgingly, continue the hard work of the ranch.

To everyone's astonishment, Boice disappeared one day, and it was years before he was home again. My mother was walking the prairie gathering bones the day he left.

I saw this rider coming, and when he passed me, I recognized Boice on the most beautiful horse on the ranch, La Mar. I yelled and yelled, and finally he stopped on a little knoll, and took off his hat, and waved it. "Where are you going, Boicie?" I asked him. "Out there, little Re, way out there" and he whirled and the dust followed him to where he was going. We never saw him on the ranch again and for years, off and on, nobody knew where he was.

Eventually, the reason for his sudden disappearance surfaced. In 1915, he and Cec had crossed over into Canada, the border close and seamless to the ranch, to hunt deer and buffalo. More than once they had gone on this venture to get meat for the family. On this particular day, they had shot a deer and were dressing it to take it home, when a ranger came upon them, pulled out his gun, and said they were under arrest for poaching. Boice, thinking they were going to be killed, shot him. Then he and Cec packed up the deer and rode as fast as they could for home. Lore has it that Boice told his father, and Albert advised him to leave immediately, and he did so. A few weeks later, there was a warrant out for his arrest in Plentywood and Scobey. Boice disappeared for a time, and the next the Chapmans heard of him, he had joined the Army and had begun writing letters home. Years later, my half-brother Jim told the story of how he and his father were in downtown Plentywood, and this bearded, straggly man came up to them. The man and Andrew talked for quite a while, and when the man left, Jim asked who he was. "That's your Uncle Boice, your mother's brother. There's a warrant out for his arrest, so he won't be around these parts long."

Losing Boice meant more hard work for everyone. Grace and Marie, with their eternal love of reading, made Maggie tight-lipped and forever frowning. Their imaginations were fired by novels, and they had endless conversations about the characters, treating them as real people in their very real world. Sometimes, they assumed names of the authors, Emily Bronte for Marie, and Charlotte Bronte for Grace. They often called each other by these names when they were growing up. All of her life my mother was an inveterate reader. It was a reprieve into the imagination, an escape from the harsh demands of life. One could abandon the tedium and hard work of the ranch into the more real world of the dream, the story.

The work days were long and tedious for everyone, especially Maggie. She was tired, exhausted, given to melodramatic outbursts and taking to her bed. By the time she was forty-two years old, she had borne ten children.

As is the way of large families, the older ones took care of the younger, and as a result, they felt they had had enough parenting to last out their days. What made the Chapmans a close family was the sense of responsibility the older boys—Cec, Boice, Coleman, and Gus—had toward the care and nurturing of the younger children and the care of the ranch. The resentment often wormed through, though, that the carefree days of their youth, as well as education and learning, had been sacrificed to the ranch and their siblings. The younger Chapmans, doing their share of hard work, didn't always appreciate, nor give credit to, the older boys.

Cecil, their mother's darling, was capable, handsome, strong, but also of a wild temperament that made the younger children in that family, especially Marie, steer clear of him. The contrast between mother Maggie's treatment of the eldest son and of Marie was obvious to everyone. When Marie was quite small, she overheard her mother say that the best reason for Marie being born was to help take care of her ailing older sister, Grace, who had tuberculosis of the bone. It hurt Marie beyond words, this casual remark, and she carried this wound with her all her days. Marie was always on the outside looking in, the solitary girl who roamed the prairie and found the dried, bleached bones of antelope, horses, cows, and buffalo, bringing them home to decorate the ranch. She was considered smart and funny, but also odd, artistic, self-willed. She smarted under the unearned spitefulness of her mother's treatment of her, and knew firsthand about unfairness and injustice in the world. All of the Chapman daughters—Marie, Ann, Eva, and Grace—felt their mother's indifference compared to the way she treated the boys, especially Cecil. This eldest, favored, handsome brother with the lightning temper and willful personality was to change the outcome of life for the Chapman family in Plentywood.

My oldest brother, your Uncle Cec, was a wild sort, not easily reckoned with and had a hot, fierce temper. It is a typical Western story of drinking, hurling insults, fighting, and gunfire. Only in this case, it was not just happening at the local bar . . . Cec was mean, and we younger kids—Billy (Eva), Ann, Jack—stayed out of his way. He liked to kick at us, chase us away, and, believe me, when he was around in a bad mood, we scampered! Sometimes in an uncontrollable fury we could hear him cursing and beating the horses, Buck and Tess, to make them do his will. You could hear their shrill, desperate whinnying, and clawing at the stalls enough to tear the barn down, their eyes rolling in their heads, bald with terror. Finally, exhausted, he quit. The poor horses, welted and sweaty, snorting and quivering with their heads down, would come to a rest. Seemed like he wanted to just beat the spirit out of them. Papa always tried to talk to Cec about horses, how much they did for us, and of course Mama would console Cec because, as she said, "He worked so hard, the poor dear." He was her golden boy, her firstborn. Papa worried about him, his temper, and I heard them talking about the way he leaned into trouble.

She paused, lit a cigarette.

He changed when he met Violet. Everything that is said about the transformative power of love was true in Cec's case. He was so smitten by her loveliness, her fun-loving nature, her delicate beauty, that he quite surprised everyone with his devotion. He married Violet when she was sixteen years old, and he was a changed man. They lived on his homestead in Dooley, and he did little things to please her—brought her flowers, helped her with household chores, and took her for long prairie rides on his horse, which she loved. When she became pregnant, he brought her to the ranch because Mama was a midwife, and could help sweet Violet who was losing her breakfast every morning, and seemed more frail than ever. I was just a girl, twelve years old, but Violet was my friend, and came with me on my prairie journeys. We laughed so much! She died of a miscarriage, hemorrhaged the life right out of her. Mama was overwhelmed by it all, especially since she was two months pregnant with her last child, my brother Dick. She watched helplessly, saw the terrible suffering of Cec and Violet, and when Violet took her last breath, Mama went to bed and stayed there for several days. We all grieved and missed her, this sweet young girl who died too soon. Young as I was, Violet's death made the whole idea of giving birth terrifying.

Her voice trailed off, lost in a reverie of another time.

I will never forget that funeral for Violet, never! Everyone in the vicinity of Plentywood was there, and the flowers! People ordered them from florists back east, and the funeral parlor was fragrant with their scent, aglow with their beauty. She was treasured by all who knew here, and sympathy for Cec and Violet's family touched the hearts of everyone. Cec, through it all, was inconsolable, and could hardly speak.

That was what the argument was all about, you see. Cec and Violet's brother, Ben Day, had bad blood between them. Violet was Ben Day's half-sister, a lot younger then he was, and he felt protective of her. He was totally against her marriage to Cec, and so this day at the bar in Dooley, drunk and in a mean mood, he told Cec that he had killed Violet, because she was never to have children. Everyone knew it would kill her. Cec said, "You knew, and didn't tell me?" Meanwhile, Ben Day was chasing Cec, hitting him over the head with a bottle, threw a chair at him, and Cec tried to escape from him. He left the bar and stopped at the store for groceries, and asked a friend there to come back with him, because he was afraid of Ben, but his friend refused. Later that day on his way home, as he passed the bar, Ben Day was still there waiting for him, drunk and crazy, and started toward him. Cec fired his gun into the sidewalk to scare him, but Day kept coming. Finally, Cec fired and hit him through the stomach. The bullet went through his hip, his bowel, and came out his buttocks. He was taken to the hospital, but it was no use.

Here my mother paused, leaning on the counter, looking at some spot out the window. I wondered if that was the end of the story, and just as I was about to get up and do my chores, she began again.

Ben Day screamed and cursed. He called for his mother, sobbing. Finally, about midnight, he whimpered into death. He had a horrible, painful ending, and everyone knew about it. It was in all the papers. Despite his mean and ugly ways, there was sympathy for him. Ben Day's family began to malign Cec, saying that Ben Day was drunk, and Cec should have understood he was not in his right mind. It marked Cec forever.

"When did all of this happen? How old were you?" I asked. She barely heard me.

It was all the news in the Plentywood Herald, *the winter of 1915. I was fourteen years old, and it was all we talked about, Cec's trial. He only spent a few days in jail, as I remember, and the jury acquitted him because of the circumstances. They called it self-defense because of Ben Day's aggression, but there were those who thought it was because everyone knew and liked Papa. But Cec was sad and empty with loss, and all those memories. He stayed* *with us at the ranch because he couldn't face going to the homestead in Dooley where he and Violet had lived. He proved up on his homestead, eventually, and enlisted in the Great War. He later sold his homestead in Dooley to Papa for $4,000—most likely to help with court costs. Cec's team of lawyers was expensive. And Ben Day's wife and family, and their battery of lawyers, were determined Cec be prosecuted.*

The lore, which circled for years, was that Cec's trial cost the family the ranch. Albert had to pay expensive lawyers, plus the court costs, and in order to do this, he had to sell some of his holdings. There were even rumors that Albert had to bribe the jury to save his son's life, but the newspaper accounts of the time belie this, and affirm that the jury concluded Cec shot Ben Day in self-defense. Years later, there were Chapman relatives who bemoaned the loss of the sweeping prairie ranch and felt deprived of their heritage on the high plains of Montana. The hard times and ceaseless struggle had been transformed, with time and telling, into a romantic, altered reality. It was the stuff of myth.

5

For Marie, life took a new turn in 1918, when she was seventeen and starting her senior year. She moved from the ranch to town to live with the C. S. Nelsons, who were friends of her parents. He was the editor of the *Plentywood Herald*, and it was here that her interest in the newspaper business began. A childless couple, the Nelsons treated her as their own. She had tender memories of Mrs. Nelson surprising her with lovely hand-made clothes, and as a special treat, often baking her favorite chocolate cake. They valued and appreciated Marie, and she thought of the Nelson home as her own. She had her own room and the attention of two people who found in her the perfect person. Nelson showed her how to set type, and he taught her to ask and answer the questions: who, where, what, why, how, and when. She quickly learned how to compose a story and set type at the same time. He was full of praise for her.

All of her stories from this time are happy ones. The news that came in and that she wrote for the paper was exciting. The borders of Plentywood shifted beyond the geography out into a larger, mysterious world through the technology of teletype that could send and receive news from around the world. That same year a rival newspaper, *The Producers News*, came to Plentywood. That event would affect Marie Chapman's life more than she could have guessed when she was seventeen years old, a senior in high school, happily living with the Nelsons and helping with the newspaper.

The Nelsons and the Chapmans were good friends, but my mother never spoke about why she left the ranch to live with the Nelsons. What is clear is that she felt free to go when her sister Grace married George Cass.

The two girls were close and often dreamed of a life beyond the ranch and the small town of Plentywood. When Grace followed her soldier husband to France, Marie had no reason to stay at the ranch. She was no longer needed. The tuberculosis of the bone, which Grace had suffered through most of her painful childhood, was still with her, but despite her discomfort,

Grace's indomitable spirit was the catalyst for her to adventure beyond the ranch. The tuberculosis had left her right leg shriveled and she had a noticeable limp, but she was in love and wanted to live her life to the fullest. The novels that Grace and Marie read all through their youth inspired them to reach out beyond the constant toil and demands of rural life into an imagined, mysterious future. With Grace married and in France, Marie's life from that time forward propelled her in different directions. She never lived on the ranch again, and had little contact with her mother.

Marie's uneasy relationship with her mother must have been one of the most compelling reasons why she wanted to leave the ranch. Her stories of her mother were never good ones, often relating how she was cold, hurtful, and demanding. Never once did my mother mention any act of kindness, sympathy, or understanding from her mother. She often mentioned her mother's criticism that she didn't do enough around the ranch, scorned her for her unending reading, and wondered who would ever marry her. Marie was, by all accounts, rebellious, inclined to question her mother's judgments, argue with her, and refuse to take orders from her. The story from my aunts through the years was that Maggie demanded they work, be dutiful, become good wives. Story after story related the distance between the mother and the daughters, but it was Marie she actively disliked. Among the Chapman siblings it was understood that Maggie was jealous of her daughters, seeing them as rivals for Albert's affection. Marie especially, because her father encouraged her learning and liked being with her, seemed to threaten Maggie the most. My mother's stories about her father illustrated how close they were, how much they shared in literature, music, and stories. She made him laugh. Albert was pleased by this unusual child, and this inspired her mother's ire. Maggie was most attentive to her first four boys, and her oldest, Cec, could do no wrong. It has been passed down through time that she told Cec's wife: "He loves you, but he loves me best of all."

6

During the World War I years of 1914-1918, life was prosperous on the Great Plains with enough rain for abundant crops and a demand for wheat to feed the troops. The Chapman boys wanted to join the fray, longing for adventure and a reprieve from the hard work of ranch life. Maggie and Albert could not stop their patriotic enthusiasm, though they were needed more than ever at home. Through good years and bad, the family had survived because of their tenacity, hard work, and perpetual hope. After Boice left, the three oldest boys, Cec, Colie, and Gus, so essential to the success of the ranch, joined the Army. One can imagine the discussions, the excitement of the boys to go on the war adventure, the worried parents seeing their boys leaving home, maybe never to return. The boys promised to write, and true to their word, the letters arrived. Their parents, Albert and Maggie, kept these cherished letters in a small linen file inherited by my mother and handed down to me.

The envelopes are gone and the letters are a hundred years old, the paper parchment thin, the pencil lettering faint with time, the wording and spelling uneducated. I like to imagine that they have been waiting in their silent retreat for history to find their thoughts, and here I am, their confidante, their Montana niece. Their simple, loving, dutiful letters mirror so many of their compatriots of that war, the many who did not return. It was a brutal war, and the Chapman boys were witness to unimaginable carnage, slaughter, and destruction. My uncles came home again, but they were changed forever from wild, eager boys into more quiet, thoughtful men. Life was fragile, death inevitable. They envisioned a horizon beyond the end of a wheat field or a Longhorn cattle drive.

The Army was not such a bad place for these men who had struggled with ranch life on the prairies of northeastern Montana and had limited schooling. One way or the other, they had been in battle most of their lives: first on the ranch, and then at the war. The war, though, took them to other places, and other possibilities. Boice, the son who was wanted for murder in Canada and Montana, the son whose father advised him to leave the country, writes as a loving and dutiful son, but also a young man looking to better himself. The letter shows him eager, full of hope, and aware that his lack of education could hold him back. There is an innocence and determination that he will and can do better. He sees the Army as a place where there are opportunities to do this. As he says, "They sent me down here to learn to be a Government inspector in the woods they say we draw one hundred and twenty five dollars a month first we have to go to school for to or three months and I am shure I'll have to improve in writing before I pass I told them I didn't have much of an education and they said that didn't matter I had lots of good common sence."

And he concludes, "Pop if I don't make good in this company it will be because it is beyond my power writing is the only thing to stop me and am going to start practicing at spare times. With love to mother and all the family, ans soon. Boice." [*sic*]

In a letter to Maggie dated March 9, 1918, from Vancouver, Washington, Coleman affirms Army life and illustrates his lack of formal schooling; it is also prescient for the future of the Chapmans, who eventually move to the West Coast: "I shure like this army so far as I have went. Its raining to beat the band today how is the weather there its all same like summer here the early plums are in bloom the lawns are all green it's a beautiful country mother when it dont rain."[*sic*]

A letter from oldest and favored son, Cec, to Maggie, dated France, March 3, 1918, finds him in the hospital with mumps, and missing his parents. "I would sure like to see you all but there is lots of weather between us wont see you for some time but that time will sure come." He ends by saying, "Hope you are well and happy, I am your loving son Cec. Give my love to all." [*sic*]

These letters resound with care and concern that the oldest boys have for their parents and for the younger children of the family they helped raise. They all survived the war, but not without injury. Cec had damaged lungs from mustard gas and had shrapnel in his leg. He also received a Silver Star and a Purple Heart, having bravely engaged in most of the serious battles of the war on the Western Front. After being discharged, he came briefly back to the ranch and, against the hopes of his parents, Maggie and Albert, announced his plans to try his luck in California. The family of the man he had killed, Ben Day, was known to be hostile to Cec, wanting revenge. The hot climate in Plentywood was not to his liking.

Coleman was in France with Cec and also had injured lungs from mustard gas. He had memorable coughing spells, and though advised to give up smoking, never did rid himself of this habit he had acquired at the age of ten when he rolled his own. After being discharged, he, too, came home to see his parents, but disappointed them with his plans to go to Wyoming.

Boice, though a wanted criminal in Montana, was able to enlist in the war and was sent to Germany. He was also injured, but not in battle. He had a fierce temper and incited a barroom brawl where he was hit over the head with a shovel and ended up in a military hospital in Germany. Luckily for him, his nurse, a lovely German girl, fell in love with his good looks and charm. He married his German nurse and moved to Chicago, never returning to the ranch in Plentywood.

Gus, the youngest of the four boys who went to war, was a successful soldier and quickly climbed in rank to sergeant. In Portland, where he was stationed, he became interested in theosophy and other religions of the world. Artistic by nature and a painter, he apprenticed to a violin maker and learned this trade, and later was able to make a living providing violins and cellos for students. An avid reader, and curious about ideas, he was often teased by the other boys as "intellectual, but not worth a damn on the ranch. Couldn't even hit a nail on the head." He came home to the drudgery of life on the ranch, and his was another voice urging the family to move to the West Coast.

Memory can select what it will, and somehow the hard ranch life was transformed through story into an idealized world where hard work and love of the land prevailed. I know as a child I viewed my mother's stories with wonder and awe. I, too, wanted to be a child of the prairie and live through those romantic hard times and survive to tell, once again, the story. It was on my first trip to Oregon and my visit to my Uncle Gus in Oswego, when I was fourteen, that this image became parallel with a more honest and real assessment. I asked my Uncle Gus if he missed Plentywood, expecting that he would spin a tale, get soft and sentimental about it all as his sister Marie did. Instead, he looked at me, took my hands in his, and told me not to worry, that it was the most god-awful life anyone could experience. "We had no childhood, no education, and no future there. There was never a time when there wasn't work to be done, and not always enough to eat. The best thing that happened to us was leaving that horrid place. No, I do not miss it, and sometimes I dream I am back there, and that is my nightmare." He urged me to read books and go to college. "You, and my two boys, your cousins, have the opportunity that I missed. You are luckier than you can imagine."

The experience of hard work and endless toil on the Montana ranch left this quiet, thoughtful man bitter at his lost youth, his lack of education.

The talk of the town the spring of 1918, the year the great war ended, was the arrival of *The Producers News* with its flamboyant editor, Charlie Taylor. He brought with him what was to be another kind of war, a war of ideas. He arrived in Plentywood, set up shop in an old livery stable, and garnered second-hand typesetting equipment from a defunct newspaper in the county.[1] Charlie Taylor was sent by the Nonpartisan League to organize the farmers around agrarian reform. The Nonpartisan League, through *The Producers News*, got the attention of the citizenry by announcing a grand family picnic they were sponsoring at Brush Lake with music, dancing, swimming, and games for children. They even promised that Montana's Jeannette Rankin, the first woman in Congress, would attend. Charlie, robust and full of energy, liked to bring people together as an organizational tool of persuasion. The picnic at lovely Brush Lake, an oasis in the desert, was a huge success, with families coming from all over Sheridan County to the tune of 6,000 people.[2]

Marie Chapman was seventeen years old at that time, living with the Nelsons, going to school, and learning the newspaper business from the *Plentywood Herald* editor, C. S. Nelson. She had dreams of a future somewhere else, and in her wildest speculations, I'm sure she did not see herself one day being involved with the radical element of *The Producers News*. The first she ever heard of Charlie Taylor was from C. S. Nelson, who told her Taylor was a "troublemaker and rabble-rouser." She had no idea then that *The Producers News* and its milieu of radicals would be her future.

While the war years brought prosperity to the Plentywood farmers and ranchers, at the war's end, the indomitable forces of nature once again assailed them. 1919 was a terrible year on the high plains for drought, wind, and crop failure. For several years, there was an exodus out of Plentywood. Many of the homesteaders abandoned or sold their claims and moved on. Many of the World War I soldiers had died in the war, or like Colie, Cec, and Gus, never came back to the harsh life of the plains. Without the boys, the Chapmans were murmuring about going to a more hospitable climate, lured on by the stories of Cec, Coleman, and Gus about the West Coast. Marie, eighteen years old, had dreams of going to St. Catherine's Academy in St. Paul, Minnesota, a school she had heard so much about.

St. Catherine's was a girls' school with a mission. At a time when education was not looked upon with particular favor for women, St. Catherine's had aspirations to be one of the best colleges in the Northwest. They had the vision that women wanted to learn and could. My mother was this kind of girl. She may have heard about this college when nuns from St. Catherine's came recruiting on the Hi-Line in Montana. Perhaps Prof Houston knew about the school through brochures, or Marie saw the ad in the St. Paul papers. Maybe it was an article in the *Plentywood Herald*. The mission of St. Catherine's was to give students a liberal education, and in doing so, train and develop their intelligence to a broad understanding of the world. It suited my mother, and was the catalyst for her artistic and intellectual development. In the words of today, we would speak of this as a "holistic" approach to education. What kind of conversation did she have with her parents about going to this Catholic school? As a Mason, her father had all the usual biases against Catholics, or "papists." My mother, though, was stubbornly determined, that girl in the photo being true to her nature. She had left the ranch and was working at the *Plentywood Herald*, living with the Nelsons, and making money of her own. She was also making her own decisions about her life.

She had always found school a reprieve from the harsh life of the ranch and her mother's demands. Prof Houston would have been a powerful ally in convincing her folks, because they liked and trusted him. St. Catherine's Academy would have been considered a safe place for Marie as a single young girl. This would have carried weight with her parents, especially her mother, who had a prurient interest in her daughters' sex lives. As they grew into young women, Maggie queried them about why they had stayed in the outhouse so long, gave dire warnings that touching themselves improperly would lead to madness and maybe even prostitution, and told them that a man wanted to marry a virtuous woman he could trust to raise his children. For Marie Chapman, going to St. Catherine's was liberation into the life of the mind and the society and culture of St. Paul.

She was, by this choice, challenging the barriers in the old social order against education for women. She was forming friendships with girls her age who wanted to learn and get an education and explore the world of possibilities. The one year that Marie attended, she studied art, music, history, and English literature. It was a year that changed her life, turning her into an advocate for women's education at a time when so few had the chance. Why Marie left St. Catherine's before she finished the college program is not clear. It may have been a money problem, or her love of journalism and wanting to return to the *Plentywood Herald*. She may also have missed her father. Whatever her reasons, the spring of 1920 she left St. Catherine's and came back to Montana, a place she carried in her heart all of her life. She was nineteen years old.

Marie was a markedly different girl when she returned to Plentywood. Now she had the air of experience about her, with her bobbed hair, latest flapper styles, and, most daring of all, smoking cigarettes. She had developed a confident, playful air, and she was a favorite in the community. Maggie was aghast, and showed her disapproval. It is telling that when Marie returned to Plentywood, she did not go back to the ranch, but returned to the Nelsons and worked at the *Plentywood Herald*. She remained with them until she got married.

9

There were stirrings among the Chapmans. During the war, Cecil, Gus, and Coleman had seen a different, more possible world on the West Coast. As the drought of June 1919 had eclipsed anything on record and the winds and fire further ravaged the landscape, people who had previously come in throngs to get the free land of the plains finally became discouraged by the weather. They were leaving in droves, abandoning their homesteads. The Chapmans hung on until 1921, convinced by the letters from Cec that the West Coast was the place to be. Maggie also missed her oldest son and was convinced, and in turn convinced Albert, they should move. They were no strangers to packing up and leaving for a better life, and the more they thought about moving to a different, easier climate, the more they warmed to the idea. They would try their luck by going even farther west, a grand adventure. When they made this decision, they had been a part of the Plentywood citizenry for twenty years.

By the early spring of 1921, the Chapman family had sold off their land, gathered what goods they deemed important enough to go to this new country, and left Plentywood. Their son Gus encouraged this new adventure farther west because he had fond memories of Portland and the coast from his Army days. He enthusiastically helped the family move, a family that included the four youngest children born in Plentywood: Jack, Ann, Eva (Billy), and Dick.

They settled in the little coastal town of Seaside, and soon after, Colie and his family left Wyoming and joined them. Colie remembered from his Army days how easy it was to grow gardens in the mild climate, the nearby ocean with its endless supply of fish and clams, the abundant wild blackberries and blueberries. This uncle with a third-grade education became a mink farmer, and knew enough about genetics to breed the sapphire mink. These pelts were made into beautiful mink coats for wealthy people back East.

There was no wishing for rain in this country or getting braced for a savage winter. In comparison to the high plains country of Montana, everything in Oregon turned to gold. For them, Montana became the land of nostalgia transformed by memory into a spare beauty, and the hardships they had endured seemed to vaporize with the hot arid winds. They never tired of missing it. For my mother, it was a separation from her family that was to last for many years. In Oregon, they knew about her, though. Bad news has a way of traveling across miles and time.

After the Chapmans uprooted and went to Oregon, Marie Chapman was without family, but she was in familiar surroundings. There is the story she loved to tell of her initiation into the Eastern Star, the women's auxiliary to the Masons, the popular organization of the solid citizenry of the town. She was to come up with something to entertain the crowd, and her choice shows a playful, even audacious confidence about her. The house party was held at the home of Adolph Reba, the town banker and prosperous farmer, with all the respectable members of the community attending. Marie came down the stairs to laughter and applause as Theda Bara, the vamp, brandishing feathers to conceal her barest of skin. Confident and fresh, she was a hit. Old friends of her family came from Outlook, Raymond, and Scobey to be present at this important occasion because her father couldn't be there.

Maybe it was at a function such as this that she met her future husband, Andrew Hansen. She was an eligible girl of twenty years old, small, pretty, lively, educated, and mischievous. When I asked her about Andrew, their courtship, she said he "had a fresh breath . . . was clean." Perhaps she said more, I don't remember. There were no stories about the beginning of their attraction, as there were later on about my father, Rodney Salisbury. Andrew was also, though she never said so, a "good catch." Rumor has it that Marie's mother was pleased when she heard her daughter was marrying this prosperous young man. He had given her an expensive diamond engagement ring. It was one of the few times she had achieved her mother's approval.

10

Andrew Hansen came from the Danish community of Dagmar, just a few miles from Plentywood. This is wheat country that stretches for miles, the golden grain swaying in the insinuating wind beneath the hot breath of summer. It is not unusual to see wheat encroaching right up to the doors of the stores, church, and houses. It means there has been enough rain, the grain has flourished, the community has prospered. Dagmar originated as a Danish community that developed various cooperative enterprises, and in the Jens Hansen family it was wheat and flour mills.

In the beginning, the town was envisioned by Emil Madsen as a religious community. Originally, in 1906, Emil came with six other people to Sheridan County and was enthusiastic about the homesteading possibilities in this country. Through the Danish newspaper, *Dannevirke*, he urged others to do what he did: get some money and a railroad boxcar, bring all their worldly goods, including animals, and settle on this spot of land in northeastern Montana. He stated in the Danish newspaper: "The colony is planned for Danish young people and those Danes with small means who cannot carry large debts, but would like to get out of the claws of the employers and away from the city's clamor and discord. Therefore we can say about this colony—the first in our history where land is distributed equally—as we say about Queen Dagmar: She came with burden. She came with peace. She came the small farmers to comfort. Signed, E. F. Madsen, St. Paul, Minnesota, 1906."

Andrew's parents, Jens and Anna Hansen, read the Danish newspaper, *Dannevirke*, and came to Dagmar, named after an honored and adored queen of their country. As early settlers, circa 1908, one of the first things they did was gather together, share what resources they could spare, and build the Lutheran church. The Vollmer church, as it was called, was built on Andrew Hansen's homestead, and his father, Jens, was a deacon there. Andrew's parents, Jens and Anna, are buried in the graveyard across from the Vollmer church. The Hansens were respected, hardworking, generous people in the community. The family came from a liberal culture in Denmark, and were comfortable with Socialist principles. They prided themselves on their integrity and cooperation. According to my brother Jim Hansen, each one in the Dagmar community knew where to go to get a threshing machine, borrow a ladder, find a rope. There was "Steam Hansen" and "Gas Hansen," two different but related families who owned combines. They were pillars of their community, prosperous, and generous with help. Because of their cooperative methods, the Danish community generally managed from year to year, despite drought and natural disasters. It was a vital part of their culture to help one another. The bank did not own them. Their machinery was paid for, or they made their payments regularly, and as Grandfather Jens Hansen said to his ten-year-old grandson, Jimmy, "We Hansens are honest men." My brother Jim never forgot his Grandfather Jens saying this to him, and often proudly repeated it.

Andrew Hansen, like most men in Dagmar, was a member of the Danish Brotherhood, a fraternal benefit society that took pride in preserving their Danish heritage not only in the present, but also for future generations. They wanted to remember and cherish their roots. Unlike the Masons, it was not a secret society, though they did attend "Lodge." The organization took care of the unfortunate by paying sick and death benefits to the survivors of those who had been ill or died. The Danish community, because of its values carried from the old country, was respected and admired. And none more so than Andrew Hansen.

Dagmar is prairie country, but has the benefit of being close to Brush Lake, an oasis in the desert. It was a popular place for locals to go and have a good time. It had a dance pavilion with jazz bands and dances that were held on those warm summer nights under a canopy of stars. Perhaps it is here Marie, a daring young flapper girl who loved to dance and laugh, met Andrew Hansen, a successful man with a dry wit, prosperous, a bachelor. Now, thinking about that marriage and the two children it made, I wish I knew more about this time. I didn't ask the right questions, and storyteller that she was, it is remarkable that my mother didn't say more. While she talked little about their courtship, she did talk about her early married life in Plentywood. Andrew had given her a ring—a large blue-cut diamond—which she wore long after the marriage had become a distasteful memory. I remember how the lamplight caught it and it sparkled, wonderfully mysterious and magical. In the impoverished years later, the ring bespoke of her life in a better time.

Marie Chapman came from respectable, solid citizenry of Plentywood. Her mother, Maggie, was the niece of President Zachary Taylor, and Marie was named after his wife, Marie Taylor. Andrew Hansen, a very eligible bachelor at thirty-two, would have known about her family, especially Cecil and the shooting of Ben Day, and Boice, who was wanted for murder. The Chapman boys were considered charming, quick to laughter, hard workers, and ready drinkers. The Chapman girls were pretty and likeable, competent, used to managing a hard life. It's safe to say that the Hansens and Chapmans knew something about each other in that small prairie community. The Masonic Lodge, to which most of the men in the community belonged, would have given them grounds for familiarity.

There is a picture of Andrew and Marie as newlyweds taken in a wheat field in Dagmar, where they were married the spring of 1922 in the Vollmer Lutheran Church. He is not much taller than she. They were two attractive, slender figures. She looks very chic in her wedding dress of white lace with black silk stockings and shoes, and her bobbed hair. They are captured by the camera, formal, somehow dutiful. They are doing what young people do—find a mate and marry. Andrew was twelve years older than his bride. He probably had many opportunities to marry before this, but there was something about Marie he liked, maybe even loved. My mother never mentioned love in reference to her husband. Living together and getting to know each other didn't foster intimacy. *He was a man's man. He could tell a joke, a story with wry understatement. People liked him. I guess I did too, for a while.*

For the honeymoon Andrew had purchased a new Ford. After the ceremony at the Vollmer church and the festivities, they went to Yellowstone Park. When I was a young girl, she told me of the wonders of Old Faithful, which shot into the air every forty-eight minutes, of the pool where you could drop your handkerchief, and it would spiral down and come back to you clean from the boiling hot pots of water. These were the prelapsarian days of a new bride. She often told stories about this journey, and one that haunts me to this day is the one where a dog fell into one of the hot pools, and its owner jumped in to rescue his dog, and both were burned to death.

Another story my mother told of her wedding trip was even more compelling.

I was with this stranger, you see . . . but a stranger I knew, and I was married to him. It was all unsettling, somehow, but not unusual, you know. . . . People got married, it was the ordinary and natural thing to do, but it just felt so strange to me. Here I was, riding in this car with my husband, Andrew Hansen. I would sleep in the same bed with him that night. I knew nothing about sex, just the facts that every farm girl knows, and the little snickers and asides, the way my brothers talked about girls who "went all the way." Mama, you couldn't ask her anything. She was more about what not to do, ever, under any circumstances, which meant don't get in trouble! I was just twenty-one years old. After I was engaged, I was with friends, and one of them said she had heard that a man's tool was big enough to hit you over the head, and you'd have a headache for days. I'm not sure I believed that, but I felt an anxious spread of dread, and curiosity, too. My life ahead would be as Mrs. Andrew Hansen. I had this large diamond ring that everyone raved about. I was supposed to have a good life, why not?

Something happened on the journey to Yellowstone, on my honeymoon, that blighted my feeling, that shrouded my marriage. When it happened, I knew the marriage was doomed, yes, doomed.

She always paused at this point in the story, leaning on the counter, lighting a cigarette, pouring another cup of coffee.

It was one of those soft, mellow days of autumn. The smell of wood smoke, old leaves, dust motes. When we passed people on the road, they'd wave at us, seeing the "Just Married" signs on the car. I remember so many smiling faces and I felt a surge of surprise, of happiness . . . How nice people were! How encouraging! We were getting closer to the park, early evening, and as we passed a farm, a beautiful Collie dog ran out, barking, and Andrew hit him. He slowed for a moment and then went on. "Aren't you going to stop?" I asked him. "The dog . . . he belongs to someone. We should stop and see if we can help him, let his family know he's been hit, maybe dead." "Oh, hell, Marie," he said. "It's just a dog and we're late already. Besides, I'm hungry."

As a young girl, every time she told this story, I felt sorry for the dog, like I always felt sorry for the horses Uncle Cec beat. The twin emotions of sadness for the animals and anger at those who abused them would leave me in tears. As I got older, there was another kind of sadness, the sadness that I felt for my mother, the young girl who lived the experiences and told the stories. Her somber tones reflected lost hope, as well as the harsh knowledge that what could have been would never be. This was not the world of *Jane Eyre* and *Wuthering Heights* and all-consuming passion. Perhaps this disappointment created in her a yearning, a feeling of loss and at the same time a freedom, a release into what new experiences might offer.

Marrying Andrew Hansen, this thirty-two-year-old bachelor, was like moving to another country. Andrew had lived in Plentywood since he was eighteen years old, and was a devoted member of the Danish community of Dagmar. Andrew's best friend was Hans Rasmussen, who was treated like a member of the Hansen family. This extraordinary man was a Socialist, a scholar, an intellectual, as well as being a mason and builder. He had been schooled in architecture in Denmark and had close ties with Andrew's parents, also from the old country. He counted as his good friends Rodney Salisbury, the sheriff of Sheridan County, and Charlie Taylor, the editor of *The Producers News*. At one time he even filled in as editor during one of Charlie Taylor's absences. This was the world that Marie Hansen had married into. As a young girl growing up in Plentywood, she was probably familiar with these families. They were a vital part of the social milieu of Plentywood, and she would have known them by reputation, and recognized them from afar. Marie, fresh from St. Paul and St. Catherine's Academy, an aspiring newspaperwoman, but with little political understanding, was in new intellectual territory. Curious, intrigued by the passionate resonance of these men and their wives, her romantic imagination was fired. This respectable girl who had worked for the *Herald*, had amused everyone with her bold Theda Bara daring at her Eastern Star debut, was open to new, original ideas. Saving the world was a good place to start, and this is what these new associations hinted at. She was open and eager to be grounded in a philosophy to live by. Young and inexperienced as she was, she had little notion as a young bride where this would take her. But take her it did, and to experiences beyond her ken when she was a young, engaged girl and then a married woman taking on the role of Andrew Hansen's wife.

They had a house in Plentywood, and their social life as a young couple was with familiar old and new friends, including the Salisburys, the Taylors, and the Rasmussens. Charlie Boulds was also a friend, as was Eric Erickson, a lawyer. They were all progressives who wanted a more equitable world for the workers. I can imagine how inspiring these people were, how exciting, for the impressionable Marie Chapman Hansen. Everything they talked about was news. She worked for the *Herald*, but was friends with *The Producers News* radicals.

A new bride, she was soon to understand what it meant being a part of the Danish community of Dagmar and Plentywood. It was all too reminiscent of life on the ranch, especially when she and Andrew helped with the busy planting and harvesting seasons on his parents' farm in Dagmar. The rest of the time he ran the flour mills in Plentywood, Wolf Point, and Scobey with his father, Jens. Her social life, spare as it was in that hardworking community, was centered on Andrew's radical friends, all older than she was. They had good times dancing to jazz bands at Brush Lake, meeting at each others homes for dinner and long conversations about politics. She also knew her father and mother, Albert and Maggie Chapman, did not approve of them and their liberal, Socialist ways.

Marie gave birth to her first son, James Albert Hansen, October 3, 1924, when she was twenty-two years old. The horrifying story often told was about the agony of that three-day birthing, during which she chewed her tongue raw. This graphic story of childbirth made me shrink from the thought of birthing babies myself. It also made Marie terrified of pregnancy, with little or no information about prevention, except for abstinence. Unlike women of today, Marie knew little about the workings of her own body. She knew, because she and her sisters were warned by their mother, that once you had your "monthlies" you could have babies. If you gave in to man's desires, you could get pregnant, and then no respectable man would want you. Being married, though, did not make childbirth easier. That she did know and had experienced.

After the birth of Jim, Marie's sisters Eva and Grace were there to help her and stayed with her several weeks until she recovered. Having babies was like being sick, to hear her tell of it. When her sisters left, she had a woman come to the house to help her with the baby, clean the house, and cook. This young mother, a future revolutionary, had all the trappings of a solid, middle-class woman. Further evidence of this was her son, Jim's, baby book, where all the leading people of Plentywood society signed their names. Andrew and Marie Hansen were popular, affluent, a charming couple. Having a baby, she soon understood, did not relieve her of the more arduous duties of farm work, however. In the planting and, especially, the harvest seasons, every family member was needed on the farm in Dagmar. The children were there, too, a part of the help at an early age.

Marie soon found out the Danish community loved their food, their coffee and pastries. Two times a year, during the planting and especially during the harvest, the days were broken up into endless meals and the tedium of constant preparation and cleanup. They rose early for a hearty breakfast before they headed for the fields. The ten o'clock coffee break was ritualized with Danish Kringle, pies, cakes, donuts, cookies. Dinner, the noon meal, followed with ham, chicken, mashed potatoes, beans, peas, corn, several kinds of bread, and finished off with pie or cake and sometimes homemade ice cream. By four o'clock on a hot day, wives and children would bring water, lemonade, coffee, and pastries out to the workers, and for a few minutes, there would be a quiet time, assessing the work done and what was left to do the next day. Finally, there was supper, leftovers from the noon dinner, ending with coffee. The days were long, fading into a mystical haze across the prairie and the solemn song of the two-noted mourning dove. Marie's value was judged by her performance, how she fit in, how she held up her share of the work.

In a letter from Marie to her mother, dated January 2, 1925, she expressed her loneliness and discontent:

January 2, 1925

Dear Mother and all,

Yesterday, I was twenty-four years old. Oh I feel so Old, so old, I took Jimmy down and had his picture taken today, but I am afraid they will not be very good as he squirmed around all the time. I had to hold him at last, I wanted one of him alone. The only word I have had from Grace was Christmas Eve, she wrote that she was in the Hospital with a tubercular abscess, I have written her almost every day since, but I haven't hear a word, Oh mama, I have worried so much over her that I feel my hair turning gray, that disease that she has is almost fatal I am afraid, I try and tell her that I know she will be well soon but I am so afraid that she never will, When I think of that poor dear old Grace and the tuff sledding that has had in the world, It makes me wish to the good lord that I could lend her a little of my good health and strength. If only I could be with her, but here I sit praying that I will hear from her, and every time I see the telegram boy coming my way I just get a hurting choking feeling, Oh I do hope that she can come home to you and have a long rest, she has been working like a man and with her health so shattered. I love you all mama and we are really coming next year if nothing happens, we are surely planning strong on it.

Oh mama, I am so tired tonite that I can hardly keep my eyes open, I am getting to hate this damn country more all the time. I wish I could be with my own people for a while, I'm tired of Daines, [sic] there are two of our neighbors coming on the train tomorrow, and they will stay until Monday. Mama it just makes me fairly hate the whole bunch, I haven't done anything but cook since Thanksgiving, and it's very little thanks that I get for it. I will close now and drop dear old grace a line Just know that I love you all mama and that I am alright because I don't get time to be anything else.

Love from all of us. Marie.

There is a melodramatic tone to this letter, and the religious overtones of her Baptist heritage. It also has the tone of a young girl, seeking some comfort, solace, from her mother. Maggie, her mother, could be quite dramatic, too. It is credited to her son Jack who said, "Mother was an actress, and had a flair for the dramatic in everyday life; even peeling potatoes could be high drama."

Aspects of married life must have been disappointing to this prairie girl whose imagination was fired by poetry, novels, music, and art. Marie viewed the world as seductive in its complexity and craved to hurl herself into the raw experience of life. At St. Catherine's, she had loved her art classes, and took to the popular art of painting china. Her gold-rimmed platters were remembered for their originality and beauty. She excelled in ancient history, art, and literature. Being married to Andrew Hansen, a member of a successful wheat farming community, had its advantages, too. As time went on, she easily took on the role of lady of the manor. She was bourgeois to the core, and at the same time, she was intrigued with the radical ideas espoused by Charlie Taylor and Sheriff Rodney Salisbury. They influenced her thinking, and she was changing.

As Andrew's wife, she could afford to hire a housekeeper who came once a week, and a seamstress who came to the house to fit her for the latest fashions. She bought silks, crepe-backed satin, delicate organdies, fine wools, and designed her own clothes from magazines like *Cosmopolitan, Ladies Home Journal,* and the *Saturday Evening Post.* When she walked downtown, she was glamorous, gracious, and kind to everyone she met.

She was accompanied by two beautiful grayhounds, adding to her air of sophistication. She was eye-catching and she knew it. With her artistic flair she furnished her modest home in Plentywood with Mohawk carpets to harmonize with walls of peach, ivory, soft greens. Warm mahogany tables and chairs, and an ornate mirror framed in silver and leaded glass, moved with us all through my childhood, as well as reproductions of Gainsborough, Rembrandt, and Van Gogh.

It was landscaping and gardening, though, that best expressed her passion for beauty and order. She often spoke of how, in the hard climate of Plentywood, she managed to raise a kitchen garden by carrying water from the house to feed it. She also kept a flower garden of tulips, zinnias, roses, columbine, gladioli, and pansies, which she nourished and tended. Though Andrew humored her artistic whims, when she mentioned a lily pond, he had reservations about its success in such extremes of weather. Marie convinced him, and he had a man come in and dig a pool for a lily pond in the backyard. To everyone's surprise, it flourished, and the neighborhood was charmed by the baby ducks that darted among the lily pads. Many years after she left that country, disgraced and out of favor, people remarked and remembered her garden. As the years eroded the neglected lily pool, it became just a faint indentation in the backyard.

12

In 1925, a year after Jim was born, Andrew began to experience head-aches, fever, and confusion. He was tired that fall and could barely make it to the farm in Dagmar for the harvest. His father was concerned, since days went by and he seemed to get no better. The local doctor thought perhaps Andrew had a brain tumor. Hans Rasmussen, Andrew's best friend, was worried, and expressed his concern to Marie, who further encouraged Andrew to go to Minneapolis and see a specialist. Finally, as his illness dragged on, Andrew's family encouraged this trip to a specialist, too. Marie, Andrew, and baby Jim boarded the train for Minneapolis. They had no idea how long they would be gone. As it turned out, Andrew was in the hospital for six weeks. While doctors determined he had no brain tumor, they surmised he suffered from a virulent flu and needed bed rest and fluids.

During the time Andrew was recuperating in the hospital, Marie stayed in a nearby hotel, visiting him several times a day. In between visits, she would put Jim in his buggy and explore the town. Interested in the culinary arts, she became fascinated with the myriad bakeries and would visit them in the morning hours, relishing the smell and sight of the delicacies displayed in the windows and behind the counters. Every day she would try a different pastry in the French, Danish, and Jewish bakeries. The bountiful choices of pastries and bread, cakes, and cookies fascinated her. Every day, she would bring a different pastry back to the hospital for Andrew. He understood about flour and would explain how the delicate texture of pastries was due to the fineness of the flour. She talked with the bakers, asking them how they were able to do their magic, and bought two pastry cookbooks. When Andrew was finally well and discharged from the hospital, they returned to Montana. Marie then practiced and became adept at making croissants, French bread, cream puffs, and Napoleans, all with flour specially milled from Hansen Flour Mills. Her culinary skills were the talk of the town; her dinner parties were gala affairs with French cuisine that she cooked herself, with a maid hired to help with the clean-up. All their revolutionary friends, like the Salisburys, Taylors, and Hans Rasmussen, showed up for these elaborate dinner parties, and there was always bootlegged booze to add to the merriment.

It was with her second child, Anneva Grace, that the situation with Andrew took another turn. Two of Marie's sisters, Ann and Grace, came to help her, and she noticed Andrew and her sister Ann were attracted to each other. She was just recovering from another hard birth, and seeing them together was painful. Marie had suspicions that they were having an affair. Andrew was a womanizer, she had discovered, so it came as no surprise to her. While everyone in Plentywood had celebrated their marriage as a great match, she was living inside it and knew it to be otherwise. I once asked her about making love as a new bride. *It wasn't much. Just rolling on and off. I always felt there was something more, but I didn't know what.* Young, disillusioned with married life and the expectations of fidelity, she turned even more to a professional life as a newspaper reporter, a stringer for the Associated Press, grateful for the interesting work that it provided. She also had the friends that came with her engagement and marriage to Andrew, the radicals that hung out in *The Producer's News* office. And there was the sheriff, Rodney Salisbury.

Womanizer that he was, there was another side to Andrew. He was there for her when she needed his support. Many years later, when we were all grown, he said to his son Jim in a rare minute of revelation, "I should never have divorced your mother. No matter how much she wanted it. I should never have let it happen . . ."

13

The newspaper business was always a happy part of Marie's life, and she was lucky to have married a man who let her explore a life outside of the married model. She was, with all of the hired help she had, free to be a professional woman as well as being a wife and mother. Andrew's sisters, Ann and Matilda, took over more of the duties of the spring planting and harvesting, with Marie occasionally helping. She was a mother with two children now, and needed to take care of them, or so she said in order to get free of some of the more tedious chores of the farm.

As a stringer, she was a freelance reporter who did individual assignments or stories. Many small outposts had stringers rather than a full-time staff member. These local stringers were useful because they had a more intimate understanding of what was happening at the local level and what was newsworthy. Marie made her rounds to the police, the sheriff, the hospital, the courthouse, the *Herald* and *The Producers News*, tracking information. If she found a newsworthy story, she would call it in to the Associated Press. She was privy to all the excitement Plentywood and the surrounding towns afforded. She loved her job, and her beat where she met and talked with everyone.

Rodney Salisbury, as the sheriff of Sheridan Country and as a friend, was one of the stops on her route. At the sheriff's office, she often met the farmers and ranchers she had grown up with talking politics with the sheriff, and points of law. The sheriff always had time for a story, a joke, or a serious conversation about best farming practices and how to get a fair share of the profits of their labors. To the businesspeople and bankers on Main Street, the sheriff and his beliefs were an irritant, a thorn in their side. To the farmers and ranchers in Plentywood, he was their friend and supporter, and they had enthusiastically voted him sheriff for his third two-year term in 1926. It was exciting for the young reporter, Marie, to be at the heart of so much political discussion. It was all new and interesting to her.

At the *Herald*, she talked with her old friend and mentor, C. S. Nelson, and the businesspeople that gathered in his office, old friends of his and her parents. She was fond of them, but found the *Herald's* rival, *The Producers News*, with the dynamic Charlie "Red Flag" Taylor, an exciting place to be. His paper was a vehicle to encourage farmers to vote for members of either party who supported state-owned grain elevators, state-owned slaughtering plants, and low-interest loans from rural credit banks. The farmers, suffering drought, low crop prices, and high rail rates, were listening. A large, hearty man with a quick wit and satirical bent, Charlie would smoke a cigar and have a drink with farmers who dropped into the paper to talk politics. It was a lively place, full of cigar smoke and laughter. It was not unusual to meet Hans Rasmussen, Rodney Salisbury, and even her own husband, Andrew, gathered around the friendly editor, smoking cigars, talking about world affairs, forming public policy.

I loved this job, and all the gossip and talk of politics, the Russian Revolution, and workers rights. We were having a great time, such an excitement in the air, the possibilities of change and fairness for folks like my Papa. It was like going to school, I was learning so much. I miss those times . . . the changes . . . Rodney and Charlie were such great friends. We all were. The farmers and workers liked and trusted them. They were great influences in the town, and there was always something happening.

Charlie Taylor had supported Rodney's run for sheriff, knowing him to be a farmer and understanding through their many conversations how dedicated he was to the Nonpartisan League and its underlying Socialist principles. Hans Rasmussen had set up a vigilante group to keep land squatters from taking a plot of land away from an absent settler. Andrew, as mill owner, wheat farmer, and member of the Danish cooperative community at Dagmar, was also a great friend of the sheriff. The two men got along well, had similar political views as Socialists, and enjoyed each other's company. They had much in common as farmers, and both subscribed to the philosophy of *The Producers News* and the Nonpartisan League that Charlie represented. *The Producers News* had a folksy tone, and one of the lead articles on the front page for August 1918 was "Vote the farmers Nonpartisan League ticket. Don't Forget!" The paper was dedicated to educating and radicalizing the farmers and giving them the power to have a say in what their labor earned. The farmers knew about hard times and understood that hard work didn't change the weather.

In 1922, the year Marie married Andrew Hansen, Rodney Salisbury, formerly the undersheriff, ran for sheriff of Sheridan County and, with the support of *The Producers News* and editor Charlie Taylor, won big. Rodney was popular, a good listener, a man quick to laughter. He was known for his generosity and easy understanding and empathy for the life of those working so hard to prove up on their homesteads, because he was one of them. He had a large sympathy for those who struggled, and he was to champion those who worked hard against the odds most of his life.

The Salisburys, Hansens, Hans Rasmussen, Charlie Boules, Erik Erickson, and other radical friends discussed politics, farming, the Russian Revolution, Lenin, and Karl Marx—all the complex changes happening day by day in their world. *The Producers News* believed in winning the farmers to their thinking through social events and education. Through the support of *The Producers News*, the year 1924 saw more people going to the polls and electing radicals who were members of the Farmer Labor Movement to most of the political positions. Rodney Salisbury was elected sheriff for the second time.

In 1924, the year that Marie gave birth to Jim, the farmers had voted so many Nonpartisan League politicians into office, that there was an air of celebration in Plentywood. To celebrate this great political victory, a venue for the local farmers and laborers was built in downtown Plentywood called the Farmer Labor Temple. Despite the split between the businesspeople and bankers and the farmers belonging to the Nonpartisan League, there was a joint effort to build a town hall, a meeting place. Many of the citizens, even those who had no interest in politics, were enthusiastic about building a community center and gave money and volunteered time. Charlie Taylor, Rodney Salisbury, and Hans Rasmussen were enthusiastic about this venture. Hans Rasmussen's knowledge of construction was useful, and he volunteered, as did Rodney Salisbury. Andrew Hansen was a generous donor. *The Producers News* stated that the community meeting place was based on "unity, not on the basis of victor and vanquished, but on the basis of real cooperation." The Farmer Labor Temple proved to be an important asset to the life of Sheridan County. Every important community event was held in the Farmer Labor Temple: lectures, youth meetings, and dances.

In their busy lives with children and earning a living, the Salisburys and the Hansens got together on important occasions, usually when something was happening at the Labor Temple. Rodney was new to Marie, a man of ideas and curiosity who was aware not just of local events, but whose knowledge extended out into the larger world that he discovered through reading. He was passionate for social justice, and worked tirelessly to bring about change. His wife, Emma, was in agreement with his ideas and supportive of his efforts. The couples' outings were fun, but also enlightening. These four engaged, curious people attended events at the Farmer Labor Temple, along with Charlie Taylor and Andrew's best friend, Hans Rasmussen. They went there to hear about Eugene Debs, methods of farming, and what the banks were doing. Afterwards, they might go to one or the other's home, drink bootlegged liquor, and talk about local events and politics far into the night, with the wafting smell of cigar smoke circling the room. It was the twentieth century, the Age of Enlightenment, the beginning of the Modern Age. People communicated across the globe by teletype and from town to town by telephone. New methods of printing made newspapers cheaper and more accessible to the masses. Information was exploding. The radicals of Plentywood, such as the Salisburys and the Hansens, were living in a volatile, interesting time, and the latest in science and medicine intrigued them, as well as Sigmund Freud and the theory of psychoanalysis, and Pablo Picasso, who changed and enhanced views on art. They were open and receptive to changes, and the zeitgeist of the times was rich in enough new ideas to keep them interested all of their lives. They were curious to know of the world beyond Plentywood, beyond North Dakota, beyond the familiar boundaries of their livelihoods. They were worldly.

My sister Camilla told me that when her mother, Emma, Rodney's wife, didn't want to go to some outing or other, she would tell him to go because, as she said, "You and Marie have such a good time." Rodney's daughter Camilla would babysit for the Hansen kids, Jim and Anneva. Along with Rodney and Marie's frequent attendance at the Farmer Labor Temple, they were also seen at Brush Lake together, dancing. They were striking, this slender woman with auburn hair wearing the latest styles, and her handsome companion, expertly swinging her around the dance floor. A romantic tune, popular in the day, was an Irving Berlin song titled, significantly, "Marie." When the jazz band played this lovely melody with its haunting lyrics, they danced. To this day, when I hear this song, it takes me back to them in all their passionate splendor, their days of wine and roses.

When Marie was sixteen and Rodney twenty-nine, strangers to each other, an event happened that was to profoundly affect their adult lives: the Russian Revolution of 1917.

It was after Anneva was born, and I was on my way to the dentist. I was crossing the street, and I met Rodney. It was the first time I saw him, really saw him, you know? I knew him, of course, we were friends. It was the way he stopped me, there in the middle of the street, leaned into me . . . like he cared. It surprised me, and I recall the moment exactly. "How are you, Marie? I hear you have a healthy baby. And you?" I told him this baby had caused some tooth problems, and I was on the way to the dentist. What was so special about him, was that he cared, the way he leaned into me, his concern, his aura, I would have to say, magnetic, powerful, promising. That encounter lingered with me. I can still relive it, exactly the way it happened.

Now when she stopped to find out the news from the sheriff, Rodney might take her with him to check out a report, follow a lead, or settle a quarrel. She enjoyed the outings, and the bootlegged beer. It was all just good fun, innocent, and in line with their work—his as sheriff, hers as a stringer for the Associated Press. They began to tell each other about their lives, their hopes, their dreams. Rodney's passion for justice and the workingman illuminated Marie's previously provincial attitudes. There was a story Rodney told her that she liked to relate, a terrifying story:

I'll never forget it. The thing is, it wasn't just a story, it really happened. These girls, young, hoping to better their lives, they were just like me, like any hopeful young person. They worked making shirts for the Triangle Shirtwaist Factory in New York. Young immigrant girls, Jewish and Italian, probably didn't even know they were being exploited. During their working day, the building was locked, they were like prisoners, you know . . . to keep them from stealing. One day, there was smoke, then people yelling Fire! Fire!

Here in the story she paused, the scratch of the match to light a cigarette a harsh sound. *There was the smoke, then the flames. Everyone panicked. They were on the eighth, ninth, and tenth floors. Some girls joined hands and jumped together, some died in the fire. Rodney said that when it happened, every paper across the states carried the headline of the March 1911 fire, and the news spread across the country like wildfire. Over one hundred women and twenty-some men were killed.*

This was the kind of exploitation that he witnessed and fought against all the days I knew him. Nobody was ever held responsible for those lives. Can you imagine? How could it be? He was twenty-three years old when this happened, but fifteen years later when he told me, it was as fresh and real as if it just occurred. He still wasn't over the injustice of it.

He told her about hard work and poverty, about books and ideas. She didn't realize it, but this was a relationship, and different from what she had with her husband, Andrew. She often said that Rodney was the first man who seemed interested in her as a person, who thought she was intelligent and interesting. It meant a lot to her. He was like Prof Houston in his interest and his caring, but more than that, too.

I stopped at his office and he wasn't there, and I felt disappointed. I expected him to be sitting at his desk, reading a book, or talking to someone who had stopped in to see him. I stood there, reading the posters on the wall: "International Red Aid," "The International Labor Defense," "The Mooney Defense Committee." I was familiar with the last poster, as he had told me about Tom Mooney, the falsely accused labor leader in jail for a set-up murder. Just as I turned to leave, he walked in, and told me he had to settle a dispute out in the country, and did I want to come along? It might be newsworthy. We got in his car and started toward Westby. On these outings, he talked to me, really talked, you know, about important things in the world: the Russian Revolution, Freud and psychoanalysis, Frederick Jackson Turner's The Frontier in American History. *He was a man of ideas, always open, always curious. I can't tell you how important this was to me, these worlds he lived in. He would tell me, "John Reed's* Ten Days That Shook the World *is one of the most important books. You must read it." He was always reading, always explaining. With him, I felt as if I were continuing my education. It was so exciting, I can't tell you.*

She always paused here in the story, lit a cigarette, opened a beer. The memory of that moment seemed to consume her.

We arrived at the place, a farm in the middle of nowhere, just endless prairie and sky, and this small shabby house. The dogs came running out,

barking. We had been drinking home brew. "Our breath . . . do you have
something?" I took a stick of spearmint gum, tore it in two, and gave him
half. At that moment, everything changed. There was something I can only
describe as "electric" between us, that instant awareness that lovers have.
"My god, Marie," he said. "What are we going to do?" He had turned white
as a sheet. "I don't know," I said. "I don't know, Rodney."

Now, aware of the outcomes of that meeting, I want to stop her, ask her, "Can you, even you, brave, stubborn, willful, talented Marie, lovely in your youth, can you do this? Can you lose it all because of this one man, charismatic, handsome, and sincere as he is? Can you defy all the pettiness and scorn of the people you have known all of your life? Can you become the subject of malicious gossip, scornful looks, the snubs of old friends? Think about this! Please stop. Be careful. You can lose it all, forever, and no going back."

I think about those two people, how they carried their anguish, while at the same time, their private worlds had utterly changed. Everything now appeared curiously bright, outlined with love and awareness. Husband, wife, children faded into a hazy background, obstacles to be sidestepped, managed. I can imagine them, dazed, getting out of the car to meet the man they were to see, to settle some quarrel the man had with a neighbor, finding it all trivial and of little consequence in comparison with this newfound knowledge that they were wearing like a heavy winter coat. How distracting, yet perhaps welcome, too. They could put off any action in the distraction of this man's conflict. Never would anything be as easy, as simple, as this, right now.

The journey back to Plentywood—did they stop, consummate this knowledge there in the hot prairie winds of a spring day in 1927? Did they surrender, in that moment of passion, all that they had been for this new discovery? I think they did, for better and worse.

15

By the time Marie and Andrew had become friends with Emma and Rodney, Charlie Taylor, Hans Rasmussen, and other radicals in Plentywood, the Salisburys already had a history. Rodney and Emma had been in the community since 1913, when they homesteaded at Raymond. Their first son, Michael, was born in 1914. Albert Chapman, as United States Land Commissioner, helped them file their homestead. At that time, Marie Chapman was a young girl, thirteen years old, living and working on the ranch, roaming the expanse of prairie around her, liking school so much she hated to miss a day, which would mean staying at home and doing her mother's bidding.

Rodney was born in 1887 in the small farming community of Pardeeville, Wisconsin, where three generations of Salisburys lived and farmed. One of my favorite stories of my father is how Solomon Salisbury, Rodney's grandfather, interested in vaudeville routines and a singer and dancer himself, took his grandson Rodney on the road with him. They traveled the Great Northern train west, and when it stopped at a station, Solomon would get everyone's attention by saying he, Solomon, was locked in the bathroom. People would hear a pounding on the door and yelling, and they would gather around to help. Once he was out of the bathroom, Solomon would laugh, introduce himself and his grandson, and give a Shakespearean soliloquy. Rodney, a boy of nine or ten, would dance an Irish jig while Solomon played a spirited tune on his harmonica. They would get a great reception, with people laughing and clapping and dropping money in the hat. Then there was the "All aboard," and those moving on would get on the train, along with Rodney and his grandfather.

Rodney as a young boy helped his grandfather get extra money along with working on the farm. By the time he had finished the fourth grade, school was in the past tense and not in his future. He could read, and his handwriting in his books is graceful and beautiful, much like the old Palmer method. I imagine what it was like for him, moving west on the

Great Northern, doing his routine with his grandfather, getting back on the train for the next stop. On the train he met a variety of people on the move, talked with them, asked questions, curious and attentive. He became familiar with the colored people who were the waiters and conductors on the train, as well as the Wobblies and itinerant workers who jumped the boxcars. Likely it is here on these trains, this touch of a larger world, that sparked this ten-year-old boy's curiosity, his admiration for characters and those seeking a better world. It was this close association with people on the move that made him at home in the world, receptive and friendly to all the stories he encountered. This world became his classroom, and he was an avid student.

Not long after this, in 1899, the Salisbury clan moved to North Dakota to homestead. Rodney was twelve years old. It was here that he grew up and eventually met Emma Ryan, a schoolteacher, and they married. I am told he proved up on his homestead in North Dakota, sold it, and decided to start his new life with his bride in Montana. His mother and father stayed in North Dakota. His mother, Alice, was to live a long life—two years beyond her son's. I think of a mother's heartbreak, knowing her oldest son had died before her.

Sometimes when I think of my grandparents, my mother and father, Andrew Hansen, the Salisburys, I tend to think of them as separate, unique individuals who happened to live in the same part of the country, the little town of Plentywood in the northeastern corner of Montana, close to the Canadian border. But as I delve into their lives, I see all the connections, their parallel yet different lives, and how everybody knew everybody. Gossip was the exciting news of the day, and everybody's business was owned by all.

16

The man my mother fell in love with had a mixed reputation, and she knew something about this. Perhaps it intrigued her more, the way some women are drawn to the outlaw, or in this case, the "scofflaw." Maybe it is the outlaws' daring, their tough intelligence shaped by hardship, giving them a vitality associated with sexual prowess and virility. Taking into account her own romantic, rebellious, and artistic nature, and her feelings stultified by the routine of motherhood and being a wife, for Marie, Rodney Salisbury was very appealing. She may also have viewed him as a liberator in the narrowest, as well as the fullest, sense. I believe they became lovers that spring of 1927. Understanding, as they must have, the perils of their passion, in those heady moments, they could not imagine the consequences that would be the result of their affair.

Through the years, old friends and acquaintances of Rodney's, who knew somehow that I was his daughter, had stories to tell about my unknown father. There was always the affirmation that he was a good and fair sheriff, egalitarian, treating everyone equally under the law. As a freshman at the University of Montana in the autumn of 1952, to help with my college expenses, I worked weekends and holidays as a waitress. I belonged to the Hotel Employees and Restaurant Employees International Union. I would often go to the union office to see what jobs were available. I don't remember how she happened to know about me personally, but the union secretary asked me if my father was Rodney Salisbury. She told me she was from Plentywood and knew him, and that he was a wonderful, generous man. "He gave my husband and me fifty dollars during the Depression so we could get married. We've never forgotten your father. He is remembered by many of us." Whenever I needed a job, she was especially kind and helpful, and whenever I saw her, she would greet me warmly and say to me, "I wish you'd known your father, Jo Anne. You would have liked him."

It was because of people like this woman that he was so enthusiastically elected sheriff of Sheridan County in 1922, 1924, and 1926. Those sheepherders and homesteaders who lived in isolation far from town welcomed a visit from the sheriff, whether in the overbearing heat of the summer, or during the hostile below-zero winds of winter. The plains country had formidable extremes of weather, with summers of stifling heat and crops withering without the reprieve of rain, and winters with harsh, unyielding storms burying cattle and sheep in a snow-driven grave. Rodney would get on his horse and ride through that tough country bringing coffee, sugar, tobacco, and a jug of whiskey to the isolated folks living on their homesteads or in sheepherder's wagons. He'd bring the latest news along with his wit and humor and enjoy their company. Lingering over a drink with them, he would match them story for story. He was a well-known and well-liked presence in Sheridan County, but he also had his enemies and detractors.

As the chief law officer of the county, part of his job was to take official notices of foreclosure from the bank and serve them to the farmers and ranchers. He knew these people as friends and, as a farmer himself, was sympathetic to their plight. When he was given a notice of foreclosure to deliver to a farmer or rancher, he would take a ride out to see them the day before, so they could hide machinery, or spread the word that there would be an auction with proceeds going to the bank. The hardworking farmers thought of the land as their own in a personal way. They organized, agreeing not to bid to the banker's benefit on the farms to be auctioned off. Anyone who did otherwise was ostracized as a traitor to the hardworking farmer. It has been recorded that a man bid one dollar, and got his farm back. Of course the bankers hated this, and they hated the man they suspected had helped with the organizing—the Socialist, Communist, Wobbly sheriff, Rodney Salisbury.

Another point of contention was Nig Collins, the owner of the local bar and brothel, the Chicken Farm, on the outskirts of Plentywood. Collins was a bootlegger, and it was rumored Rodney was lax about this, and indeed, bootlegged himself. Plentywood was close to the Canadian border, and it was an easy haul to acquire the forbidden booze from Canada and transport it to Plentywood. It appeared that many people were involved in bootlegging, and there were complaints by federal authorities that Rodney was not being vigilant enough in curbing this illegal traffic. The Sheridan Council of Action, Progressive Farmers of Montana, heard the allegations against Rodney and, chaired by Hans Rasmussen, did a thorough investigation. As reported in the following article from the *Helena Daily Independent*, dated January 30, 1926: "We find no wrong-doing on the part of the Sheridan County officials." The council further stated: "We find that the County Attorney and sheriff have arrested and convicted a larger number of liquor law violators in this district than any officers holding similar positions in any of the nearby counties," and that "at the present moment the jails are filled to capacity with men who were convicted of violating the state law and their places of business are closed by injunction."

The paper went on to say, too, that the Council of Action, Progressive Farmers of Montana, was a secret organization supported by *The Producers News*. With Hans Rasmussen, Andrew Hansen, and Charlie Taylor chairing this committee, it would be easy to see a favorable bias.

As the sheriff, Rodney was not judgmental of prostitutes and understood the economic necessity that drove women to this kind of work. They had a clientele of locals that kept it going, many of them respectable married men. For Rodney, the economics of capitalism absorbed everyone, and he placed no blame on these women, but more on the system that gave no place to women in the hierarchy of political and economic life. He also saw marriage for economic security as another kind of prostitution, and just as degrading. He knew many of the people who frequented the Chicken Farm, and noted their hypocrisy. Because he was a representative of the law, some people expressed outrage that he didn't do more to curb illegal activity there. When things became too rowdy at the Chicken Farm, Rodney would go in and give a warning. Eventually, there was such an outcry by the locals against the Chicken Farm and its unsavory reputation that it was closed down. In an ironic twist, Nig Collins, before he left town, deeded the Chicken Farm to Rodney Salisbury.

My sister Camilla had an interesting story about the Chicken Farm. The madam of the brothel, Maisie, needed temporary housing until she could relocate. Rodney approached Emma about Maisie staying at the ranch for a while, and Emma agreed. Camilla told me wonderful stories about how

Maisie had a bird in a cage, wore lovely clothes, and was jolly and fun. She helped with the household chores, weeded the garden, and above all, loved to ride the horses. The Salisbury children often rode with her, exploring the vast prairie. One day, a handsome man drove up and put all of her belongings in his car. He said they were headed west. Maisie hugged everyone and cried. She promised she would write as soon as they got settled. The car took off down the dirt road with the Salisbury kids running after it, yelling goodbye, and Maisie waving to them with a handkerchief out the car window. They never heard from her again, and yet so many years later, when Camilla spoke of her, it was with affection and good humor.

Rodney's reputation, it can be fairly said, was mixed between scofflaw and saint. Those who knew him well found him a true friend, a good listener, and non-judgmental. He had a fondness for characters, those who were eccentric with a bit of an edge and held different opinions. When the Industrial Workers of the World, the "Wobblies," came to town looking for work, they could count on a meal and could stay overnight in the jail, if they had nowhere else to go. They organized on the job and were a member-run union for better working conditions, and Rodney paid his dues and joined. These men from all over Eastern Europe had many stories of the hardships and injustices they had encountered in their work worlds, and they influenced and furthered his own sense of injustice.

In November of 1926, while Rodney was serving his third term as sheriff, the courthouse was robbed. All the tax receipts, cash and checks valued over $100,000 were taken. Two masked robbers entered the courthouse, tied up the county treasurer and his deputy, and locked them in the safe. They were discovered an hour later, and by that time, the robbers were long gone. Rodney, as the sheriff, was in charge of the investigation. It was his job to find the culprits and bring them to justice. According to my mother, Marie, he had a lot of ideas about who had done it, but no proof. The rumor circulated rather quickly, with help from the *Plentywood Herald*, that it was an "inside job," and Rodney was suspected. *The Producers News* and its editor, Charlie "Red Flag" Taylor, supported him, extolling the great job he was doing fighting crime in Plentywood.

Marie and Andrew heard all the rumors about the robbery being an "inside job," and that Rodney may have been one of the ringleaders. I remember her saying that he felt sure he knew who had done the robbery, but he had little proof, and had he followed through on whom he suspected, the man was too powerful in the town to be convicted. That's the only thing I remember her saying. It has been suggested to me that perhaps she was protecting him, that she knew more than she was telling. They were close, and this could be true, but if she knew he did the robbery, she kept his secret. I know it was not one of her stories about him, and important events for my mother meant a story, a memory, called forth again and again. Those were always the stories that framed her experience, that shaped her life. They were her truth.

In our later years, after my sister Camilla and I became friends, I mentioned the courthouse robbery. I asked her if Rodney as sheriff had done it. She laughed. "Of course he didn't rob the courthouse, but he was the perfect fall guy. I have a theory. You know, during the robbery Anna Hovet, the deputy treasurer, was tied up, and put in the vault? Well, she was also the "nanny" of the banker and great landowner, Adolphe Reba. She lived with the Rebas, and rumors were circling about that his bank was in trouble. I speculate she could have had something to do with this robbery, and the money went to his bank, to keep him solvent. When he died, he left her that big house and the land around it. Course, everyone suspected she was more than just a nanny, you know."

I have passed this story on to several folks who are descendants of people who lived in Plentywood at that time. They see some validity in it. Rodney and Emma's children, the ones I knew—Mike, Gene, Camilla, and Jardis—spoke always of their father as an honest man, respectful of the law. I never had the good fortune to have that ready bias. I was too young when he died. His legacy to me is his library, stories from my mother, brothers, sisters, and old friends, and sometimes, damaging newspaper accounts.

In a small town like Plentywood, where news travels faster than smoke signals, people knew Rodney and Marie were meeting, but never knew where, though there were "sightings." It was rumored they were seen coming out of a hotel in Minot, North Dakota. Someone else saw them in the early morning driving into town. Another rumor had them parked by Brush Lake in the early hours of the morning. In all the stories my mother told me, she never mentioned specifically where their liaisons took place. Hotels out of town would be my first guess. But I can also see them taking blankets and pillows from the back of the car, placing them on the sweet grass by Brush Lake, talking and laughing as they watched the sun go down and the surreal haze of the prairie fade into the quiet gloaming. The only sound the tender lapping of the lake waves, they turned to each other. There under the diamond sky and friendly moon, they knew love. (As I write this, I can hear my mother's easy laughter, her favorite quote of Keats: *Oh, Pet, The only truth is the truth of the imagination!*)

My brother Jim remembers Rodney coming to the Plentywood house, but since the families were friends, that would not have been unusual. He also mentioned many times when speaking about his early years that his mother wasn't around much. Marie said she and Rodney were together for thirteen years before he died, so that would mean they started seeing each other in 1926, soon after Anneva was born. I do know that they plotted how to get away together. I can imagine Marie made excuses to Andrew about where she was going, usually something to do with her job as a stringer, and the housekeeper took care of her two children, two-year-old Jim and baby Anneva. As for Andrew, he was busy with the flour mills and also with helping out on the family farm in Dagmar.

It's easy to imagine the besotted lovers were figuring out ways to be together without rousing the suspicion of their respective spouses, Andrew and Emma. Infidelity carries with it a complex, secretive world festooned with plans for rendezvous, intimate clandestine meetings, the telling of elaborate lies. Only once did I see a letter that my mother wrote to her lover Rodney: "I have a rendezvous with love," by paraphrasing the Alan Seeger poem, "I have a rendezvous with death," which also had its metaphoric reality. My mother's bourgeois world was challenged by the passion for this one man who influenced her intellect and emotions until the day she died.

Marie knew from their many conversations that Rodney's radicalism was an important and vital part of his life and heritage. His passion and eloquence about economic justice enthralled her, and she took it on as her own. His father, Henry Ward Beecher Salisbury, was named after the abolitionist brother of Harriet Beecher Stowe, author of *Uncle Tom's Cabin*. This was Rodney's heritage from his grandfather, Solomon, to his father, Ward. I can imagine that the oppressive system of capitalism, which used slave labor, exploited workers, and had free land taken from Indian tribes, was the historical truth of his time. The Russian Revolution of 1917 captured his imagination and showed that oppressive institutions could be uprooted, if people organized. Rodney always imagined a better world, brought about by education and struggle and grounded in understanding and empathy. Rodney and Marie saw themselves as working and waiting for the revolution, and their model was the Russian Revolution of 1917, which liberated the peasants and got rid of the oppressive monarchy. When the revolution happened, Marie was sixteen, a dreamy girl reading poetry and novels and roaming the prairie between school and work on the ranch. Rodney was a twenty-nine-year-old man, radicalized by experience, married with a family, and intrigued by what had happened to the monarchy in Russia. It is said that Europe was so liberal and understood the plight of the Russian people so well, that no country wanted to give exile to Czar Nicholas. The Russian Revolution had not only a powerful affect on the world, but on individual imaginations as well. Rodney Salisbury was one of those individuals.

From such a model people envisioned the possibility of worldwide revolution, a sort of domino effect. This was the Marxian ideal, Lenin's hope, the model that Russia offered the world. The larger world of injustice and oppression was the canopy under which these two individuals, Rodney Salisbury and Marie Chapman Hansen, loved and worked together for a more just system for workers, farmers, women, the poor, and the oppressed. The passion for action to bring about a better world was often at odds, not with their devotion and passion for each other, but with the responsibilities, grave and necessary, to which they were also committed: their families.

17

When their affair began in 1926, they both had very young children: Rodney's were cared for by his wife and the older kids who helped out, and Marie's were cared for by a variety of housekeepers. Rodney and his wife, Emma, had six children. In 1926, their oldest son, Mike, was thirteen, Eugene was eleven, the twins, Jardis and Janice, were nine, Camilla was six, and Patrick was two years old, a toddler. In those formative years of their young lives, their father was a scarce presence. As a farmer, organizer, sheriff, and a man who was in love with another man's wife, he was gone many days of the week. Before the affair was known, when the families were still friends, the twins often took care of the Hansen kids when their parents went on an outing together.

Marie and Andrew's son, Jim, was two, and Anneva was a baby when Marie was emotionally and mentally absent. She had the passionate distraction of a lover and a whole new philosophy of life. The world beckoned from the outer rims. She and Rodney were totally engaged in bringing about change for economic and political justice. They had many examples of the oppressive capitalist system: the way union organizers were killed, the oppressive life of factory workers, the broken promises to the Indian tribes. As for their children, there was always somebody there to take care of their physical needs.

Between their passion for justice and all the activities they helped organize and attended at the Farmer Labor Temple, they must have known their absence was hard on their children, all young enough to need their parents. It was for Rodney and Marie a moral dilemma and fraught with guilt, driving them to dutifully be with their families. These necessary separations they endured, going to their respective homes, being with their children, taking care of household chores. They maintained their separate households and kept up appearances for years. Emma often scolded Rodney about his long absences, but when he was home, he spent time with his children and enjoyed them. Never, in all the time I knew them, did Rodney and Emma's children say a word against their father. To them, he was a wise, caring, and honest man.

For my mother, it was different. Being home with her children meant being with Andrew. As time passed, she felt the oppression of being married to this man while loving another. All of their caution at the beginning of their relationship couldn't be maintained. Eventually, rumors began circulating, suspicious looks came their way, and their discretion failed them. I think of love and romance, and how it affects people in the throes of it. There is that special look, the brief touch, the unself-conscious conversations, the intimate laughter. As time went on, they seemed to care less and less what people thought or said, or perhaps they were simply oblivious. They were on a mission for justice, they were in love, and that was all-consuming.

It must have been after a year of their clandestine meetings that the Plentywood citizenry began to whisper. When people began to suspect Marie was having an affair with the Communist sheriff, the community's conventional wisdom of married faithfulness and Christian ideals was affronted.

Thinking of my mother living in this small town of Plentywood, having an affair with the sheriff, Rodney Salisbury, with rumors flying, takes me back to some years ago, and how the past can be called up so easily, especially when the tale is worth telling.

I am married, living in Bozeman with my husband, Vern, and our small daughter, Allison. It is 1972. Our daughter's babysitter is a friend from college, and she has invited a group of us to her house for dinner. Her mother and stepfather are also going to be there and she wants us to meet them. It is a lovely autumn day, and we are in the backyard drinking wine and enjoying the ambiance of the lovely garden. I approach our hostess's mother, and we begin a conversation. She tells me, much to my surprise, that she is from Plentywood, that she grew up there. "Did you know my father, Rodney Salisbury?" I ask. It's partly innocent and partly curiosity: what will she say about this controversial Communist sheriff of Sheridan County?

"Oh, his wife, your mother, was a saint, but that woman he took up with! A married woman with two children, just babies, stepping out on her husband! Brazen, they were, and showing up everywhere just as pretty as you please! She was big pregnant with his child, the whole town knew it. She came into the post office, cheery, as if nothing were wrong, saying hello to all of us. Nervy! We were so shocked to see her, flaunting her big belly, we couldn't say a word. I remember her, all right. She stared at us all, and said (oh, the brazen defiance of her!), 'I believe in free love.' She flounced out and slammed that door. Well, I can tell you, we had a lot to say about her and her 'free love.'"

I smiled, made some inane, noncommittal remark, and we sat down to dinner. At some point in that dinner, I glanced at her, wondering about the antagonism that had lasted through the years for this pregnant woman in the post office of Plentywood. Our eyes met, and then something happened. I could tell by the horror-stricken look on her face. She had figured it out: that woman, the brazen, impetuous free lover, was my mother. The story she told made sense to me, and was also a revelation about "that woman," my mother, cornered in the post office by the harpies of the town. All of her defiance and surety about love and romance had come to that moment of truth: she was an outcast, a pariah, she who had once been a secure and privileged person in her hometown. She began to question her. position as the mistress of Rodney. Likely the idea of free love began to pall as the reality of living as a scorned woman became more intolerable for her. At some point in their relationship, Rodney agreed to try and get a divorce from Emma, and Marie agreed to get a divorce from Andrew.

These many years later, in thinking of my mother, I see how her defiant response was that of a stricken, vulnerable woman. She was hurt, forever separated from her familiar, safe, and conventional world, and in those few minutes in the post office, she knew it. She also must have known there was no going back.

From my mother's stories, Rodney and Marie were intimate people who confided everything in each other. I can imagine the scenarios that resulted from the discrimination she felt at times. My mother was ever expressive, having a bent for the dramatic, and she would have talked with Rodney about how she was being treated, and how it made her feel. In that unfair but ironbound world of preconceived gender roles and the double standard it supported, he was not getting the same treatment, though there were people who were decidedly critical of him. I can easily imagine there were times when she broke down and cried, hurt and angry, and Rodney would have consoled her, told her the opinion of narrow-minded people didn't count.

At the same time, I'm sure she felt above it all, a bit arrogant in her intellectual loftiness. She was flaunting her newfound freedom. Rather than a loveless marriage, she was opting for an authentic existence based, not on propriety, but on her particular reality. She was to find that she did not get much admiration for her integrity in this matter. She did, though, have a few who stood up for her, who understood and sympathized, and those few remained friends of hers for years after she left Plentywood.

18

As a married woman, Marie was disappointed. She was a romantic, believing in love as some ultimate state of being, a soul connection where two people could intuit what the other was thinking. Above all, they were true to each other, and weathered any obstacles to be together. Her favorite novels as a girl were *Wuthering Heights* and *Jane Eyre*. She loved the romantic poets and had memorized her favorite poems from Keats, Shelly, Wordsworth, and Coleridge. She was dramatic; she had flair and a lively imagination. She was quirky, and some absurd bit of humor would send her into gales of helpless laughter. This was the woman Rodney knew and loved.

Rodney, thirteen years older than Marie, handsome and articulate, intrigued her with his wide range of knowledge. Always alive to new ideas, Rodney was attracted to the anarchists, especially one of the most famous, Emma Goldman. She was the queen of the anarchists, and dubbed "the most dangerous woman in America" for her beliefs. She espoused free love, a convincing argument based on her observation that marriage was largely an economic arrangement and did not necessarily have anything to do with love, but was more a submission to the conventional. In Emma Goldman's philosophy, love and passion were individual, a matter of emotional bonding and intimacy, having nothing to do with religion or the state. Most people, Goldman asserted, lived in the conventions of a loveless marriage, in a farce, not having the courage to buck public opinion. An anarchist always, she had a special lecture about this, and in her articulate, logical way, it made sense. The people in her audiences who had married because that was the norm, often felt the truth of her philosophy. In the 1920s and 1930s, especially in rural America, the options for women were limited. A woman could be a nurse, a teacher, stay home and care for elderly parents, or go into a nunnery. Or they could marry. Being single, a spinster, was a loaded, almost accusatory word. People married young, and could find themselves one morning with several children, sitting across from a person they didn't know very well, a stranger, maybe even someone they didn't like but had to endure. Goldman's ideas appealed and made sense to many people who saw her unconventional ideas as liberating and true to a reality they were experiencing. Rodney was certainly one of those people.

For Rodney, espousing free love meant not only believing in it, but following through by acting on this belief. It probably wasn't too difficult to convince my mother, who could see the sense of it, herself being in one of those rather loveless marriages that Emma Goldman described. Emotionally and intellectually, she wanted to live an authentic life, rather than a charade. Her romantic disposition would have seen the obstacles they encountered as simply the course that true love had to take. At least, I conjecture, in the early passion of their relationship, this would have been her grounding.

For Marie, falling in love with the charismatic sheriff of Sheridan County was fraught with peril on many counts. They were both married and entrenched in the small-town society of Plentywood on the prairie. Both Emma and Marie were liked by all who knew them; they were good friends, and both families had small children. For Marie's part, the intensity and focus of her feelings barely touched upon Andrew, her children, and her marriage vows to him. She had an intellectual, as well as emotional, basis for her feelings, all authenticated by the free love philosophy and, most of all, by Rodney, who was willing to venture out into the deep waters of infidelity with her. I can imagine, in sober moments, how she rationalized her situation with Andrew, claiming justification because he was a womanizer. As far as she could see, he didn't seem to care that much about her or he wouldn't be such a philanderer. As the future was to show, his relationship with his wife, Marie, was more complicated than she rationalized.

It is hard to keep secrets in a village where the most interesting news is what other people are doing. A year into their affair, rumors were chasing the latest news of Rodney and Marie's whereabouts and what they were doing. They seemed unable to conceal their affection for one another, or practice the discretion necessary for two people so well-known and liked in this small community. What I do know, counting backward, is that by January 1928, when her daughter, Anneva, was about a year and a half old, Marie was pregnant. She and Rodney had been together a little over a year.

Your honor, years ago I recognized my kinship with all living beings, and I made up my mind then that I was not one bit better than the meanest on earth. I said then, and I say now, that while there is a lower class, I am in it; and while there is a criminal element, am of it; and while there is a soul in prison, I am not free. Eugene Debs[3]

On a rainy autumn afternoon in 1948, there was a knock on the door, and there stood my half-brother Mike Salisbury. He was Rodney's oldest son, the jazz piano player. I was fifteen years old and had never met him. He was thirty-five, witty and fun, and we became instant buddies. He wanted me to know about my father, and he once read the above statement to me. "This guy, this Socialist, Eugene V. Debs was your papa's hero. He was a great union organizer, worked for the railroad, and called a strike against the railroad tycoon, Pullman. Of course they called in their goons and broke the strike and arrested Debs. See, kid, Debs was like your Dad. Had to quit school to support his family, saw the miseries of working people, wanted to do something about it. Ran for president on the Socialist ticket, and we voted for him. Remember this quote, girl. This is Debs, but it is your papa too."

My mother spoke to this idea once that I remember, but she may also have reiterated it many times, as she did so many of her stories. It seeded itself in my brain, and to this day I can remember the time, the location, the surroundings of her striking utterance. It was autumn, and I was sitting at the table doing my homework; she was canning. I asked her something about class, what it means.

Do people with money have more class than those who don't, you ask? That is an important question, Jode. Remember, if you have culture, if you have a passion for learning, for art, literature, music, history, science, philosophy, you are in a class of your own. You can go anywhere with that. If you just have money and are ignorant of the world, or don't care about anything but yourself, then your ignorance will be your class.

She hesitated here, lit a cigarette, and then she said, *Your father once said to me, "Because of the choices we have made, Marie, we are classless." He meant this in a more literal sense. Do you understand what I mean?*

Even now, I remember what her face looked like when she said that. She seemed inscrutable to me, a thought hidden behind a flat look. What did quoting my father remind her of? Perhaps what she had given up to be with him? Did she not dare utter the possibility that the free love, the classless state she took on, also meant poverty and the ignorant disdain of her by people wedded to the conventional mores of the times?

That is my heritage, my legacy from my mother and father. I like to think of myself as classless and, like Debs, recognize, as my father did, "my kinship with all living beings." It is an idea I strive for, not always with success.

A Socialist and an articulate, convincing speaker, Debs made this statement to the court in 1918, speaking against American participation in World War I. This led to his arrest and conviction under the Sedition Act of 1918. He was sentenced to a ten-year term in prison. At that time, my father Rodney was thirty years old. Like Debs, he didn't believe in the war, and would have been a conscientious objector. However, with the birth of the twins, Janis and Jardis, and as a farmer, he was exempt from the draft. From an early age, when he was in North Dakota, Rodney was an admirer and follower of Debs's Socialism. His first voting experience for president when he was twenty-four years old was for Debs. He voted for Debs every year that he ran, the last time in 1920 when Debs was in jail. According to Marie, he joined the crowds who listened to Socialist speakers whenever he could. He subscribed to the Socialist weekly newspaper, *Appeal to Reason.* (I know this, because many years ago when I was a young girl, I found copies of the paper in an old suitcase of his in the attic.)

At the same time, a Socialist mayor was voted into office in Butte, Montana. The success of Socialism, in a minor way, was a protest against the two main political parties. There was the idea that what Debs wanted was to replace the existing order with a more equitable system, a cooperative system. He wanted to clarify to the working class the "contradiction between the reality of industrialized capitalism and the promise of life."[4] Debs did not look at the problem as a class struggle. He envisioned the middle class and working class as embracing Socialism in the spirit of the Declaration of Independence.[5]

Charlie Taylor, hired by the Nonpartisan League to start *The Producers News* in Plentywood in 1918, was another important man who further radicalized Rodney. His paper emphasized organizing and educating farmers to fight for their rights. The *Plentywood Herald* was persistent in its stalwart position against all *The Producers News* stood for. Now, as I see this as part of the historical record, I am curious that my mother didn't choose to detail this in any of her memories of Plentywood. When she mentioned the *Herald*, it was always about when she first moved in with the editor and his wife when she was a young woman and learned the art and craft of writing newspaper articles. The Nelsons were good to her. It was said that she worked for *The Producers News*, but that is in error. She may have helped write articles for the *News*, and certainly she would have been a staunch defender of *The Producers News* because she was in love with a man who was closely associated with it. She was grateful for the opportunity the *Plentywood Herald* and its editor had in establishing her journalistic career, but her sympathies were with the philosophy of *The Producers News.*

Rodney met Charlie Taylor shortly after Taylor arrived in Plentywood in 1918, when my mother was a senior in high school. At that time, Rodney was the undersheriff. Both men at first acquaintance found that they had much in common: they both were fathers with young families; both were progressive thinkers who were engaged in world events; both were interested in the Nonpartisan League with its close ties to American Socialism, and how they could organize the local farmers. They shared a common interest in the works of Karl Marx and Frederick Engels, and both were excited by the hope for a new age ushered in by the Russian Revolution of 1917. They and countless other liberals, free thinkers, Socialists, and anarchists were living in the shadow and light of that unusual time. It had motivated them to advance the ideas of a more equitable society, free from exploitation, and against the abuses of capitalism. It is easy to see why these two men, important and influential in Sheridan County, one the editor of the paper, and the other an undersheriff, would form an abiding friendship. Between the two of them, they could wield a powerful influence in achieving their utopian goals in Plentywood and, by organizing, throughout the United States.

Taylor was drawn to Rodney, because he saw him as charismatic, a great organizer, and intensely interested in the political message of . Taylor, with his worldly experience and education, saw Plentywood as a small, backwater town. It was individuals such as Rodney Salisbury, Hans Rasmussen, Andrew Hansen, and the lawyer, Eric Erickson, who made this adventure into the small town and lives of Plentywood more acceptable, more hopeful. Soon, they were meeting at one another's homes and, over bootlegged whiskey and cigars, discussing books such as Upton Sinclair's *The Jungle*, Willa Cather's *O Pioneers!* as well as their dreams for social justice. Like-minded, they were becoming intimate friends, and totally sincere in their revolutionary aims. Rodney was often seen at *The Producers News*, helping Charlie with information and taking a hand at writing articles himself.

Charlie was a big, voluble man at ease with working people, a man who liked a stiff snort of whiskey and a good cigar. As the Nonpartisan League representative in Plentywood, he had ideas about what farmers needed, and he, like Rodney, was a great community organizer. Rodney and Hans Rasmussen helped Charlie organize the Nonpartisan League picnic that first spring of 1918. Charlie played it up big in *The Producers News*, and folks from all over Sheridan County and beyond attended the festivities at Brush Lake, not too far from the Danish community of Dagmar. There was a dance pavilion, a beach for games and swimming, and food provided by the Nonpartisan League. Folks arrived in a holiday spirit that first year, eager to have a good time. An added incentive was the prospect of Jeannette Rankin's visit to the picnic, though she had to cancel. Six thousand people showed up and had a memorable time, among them, members of the Chapman family. It was talked about for years afterward.

Charlie was the right man for the time, and *The Producers News*, with the motto, "A paper of the people, by the people, for the people," was lively and full of information for farmers. There were always notices in the paper of meetings where farmers could get to the facts of their situation. "Small Town Kaisers Get Some Jolt from Organized Farmers," was the headline for April 26, 1918. "Insurance Men to Fight Farmers' League," got top billing for May 31, 1918. "Miles City Has Gone Stark Mad," avowed the May 17, 1918 edition. The tantalizing headline for May 19, 1918 was an invitation into the "Story of the Swinish Hog Island Paytriots." Charlie knew how to both interest his readers and inform them. The paper was so popular that within two years it had a circulation of 2,500 in Sheridan County, which had a total population of 12,000.[6]

That next year, 1919, had one of the worst droughts recorded in Sheridan County, and many farmers struggled to make ends meet. Charlie Taylor, as editor of *The Producers News*, could write about their plight. Taylor was not a farmer, but Rodney, who was, understood what was happening—the mortgages with the banks, the desperation of hardworking people in a chancy climate. Together, they were to wield a great influence on the community.

While all of this was happening, Marie Chapman was living with the Nelsons, working at the *Plentywood Herald*, and getting ready to graduate from high school. She was dreaming about moving to the city of St. Paul, and attending college at St. Catherine's Academy.

20

As Marie saw it, Rodney Salisbury seemed to have the pulse on every new trend that appealed to social justice and that was opposed to the capitalist system. Rodney knew about "Big Bill" Haywood, who was an imposing, colorful figure with a confident booming voice. In 1905, he was one of the prime organizers behind the Industrial Workers of the World, the "Wobblies." He was appealing in his rowdiness, his working-class experience as a cowboy, a miner, a homesteader. He was a man of conviction and could extend a reasoned argument with that strong voice that appealed to workers. They trusted him. He had been a member of the American Federation of Labor, but soon came to mistrust the A F of L because he saw it as a tool for the capitalist system. He viewed the worker under capitalism as a "wage slave." Rodney identified with his radicalism and his total mistrust of the capitalist system, and joined the IWW. He and "Big Bill" were both "scofflaws," scoffing at laws that were tools of the capitalist system, and proud of it. The Wobblies were anarchists, believing in direct, immediate action to change the system. They used the force of strikes. Nothing was more contemptible to them than a "scab," a worker who would walk through a picket line. The Wobblies rode the rails and came to the farm country of eastern Montana, looking for work in the wheat fields. One of the favorite, legendary Wobblies of the time was Pete Steinov, who worked for various farmers in the area, including Rodney, Andrew, and Charlie Taylor. Ever faithful, Pete came seasonally for many years, and was a familiar figure around Plentywood.

Marie, smoking, leaning on the counter on a rainy autumn afternoon, spoke fondly of Pete:

Pete Steinov was from Bulgaria, a proud member of the Industrial Workers of the World. He came to town and got jobs on Rodney's farm, planting and harvesting, and also worked for the Hansen family in Dagmar. Oh, he was a character, all right, and Rodney loved characters, you know. I never heard Pete mention a family, whether here or in Bulgaria. He was, like so many of his kind, an iterant worker, homeless, going from place to place, riding the rails, jumping a boxcar. He was sturdy, strong as an ox, a dependable worker. It was Pete that started calling our son The Budson, and the name stuck. He carried gossip from household to household, and did this for years, and it made us laugh. We always looked for him to arrive sometime in the spring and stay as long as there was a job. He was a favorite of Charlie Taylor's too, and of course Pete was an old Communist/Socialist, radicalized by his life as an itinerant worker, and also as a foreigner to whom this country had held such promise, but which he never quite realized. He followed our separate families all through the years, even when we had all changed households and left Plentywood. In his own way, he was being loyal to all of us with his visits, letting each family know what the others were doing. He was an endless fount of information, most of it more or less accurate. I never heard him mention any family of his own, so I think we all took the place of family for him.

Here she laughed, and lit another cigarette.

He also realized the interaction between the families was sometimes hostile, so he would be sure to include something awful about Leora, my old housekeeper, who was now Andrew's wife, or that Emma's garden was a failure. He knew I liked these negative stories about them.

She hesitated here, lost in some faraway place in Plentywood, maybe, or thinking about her own life, and what Pete would tell those families.

21

Howard Froberg "Budson" Judson Douglas Hansen was born on September 4, 1928. At that time, Marie was living with Andrew and their two children, Anneva and Jim. When this third child was born in the Plentywood hospital, Andrew Hansen, as Marie's legal husband, signed that he was the father. There is some mystery surrounding this. My mother knew who this child's father was, Rodney Salisbury. There never was any doubt in her mind; however, there were murmured suspicions by people of the community that Andrew Hansen believed that this child was his. Whatever knowledge was afloat, Andrew Hansen treated "Budson" as his own son, though people talked.

I have always wondered if Andrew signed that he was the father to protect his vulnerable wife. Or did he do it out of vanity, to save face, unable to have people know that his wife had taken up with another man? Or did he believe this child was his? At any rate, Budson spent the first five years of his life living in Plentywood with Andrew, Marie, and his brother and sister, Jim and Anneva. Little did any of the adult players understand, nor could they predict, how this would affect him all of his life.

Rodney and Marie were still often seen together at the Labor Temple. They would sometimes take their children with them, Budson included. As Budson grew into a little boy, it soon became evident that he looked like his father, Rodney, not his legal father, Andrew. This, and the fact that Marie and Rodney were becoming more open about their relationship, set the town astir, and gossip about them flourished. Perhaps they assumed the lofty position that this was free love, after all, with its core belief that only individuals could determine whom they loved and wanted to live with. With this understanding, they may have rationalized that they were not bound by the ordinary conventions that imprisoned one in hollow, meaningless, albeit legal, marriages.

There is one story that my mother told that always intrigued me as her young listener. It had to do with another boy, a little older than Budson, who was also Rodney's son.

We were walking down the street in Plentywood, Rodney and I, holding Budson between us. Coming toward us was Alice Young, now married to Orville Iverson, with her son, a boy a little older than Budson. We all said hello, and after we had crossed the street, Rodney turned to me and said, "That little boy with Alice, he's my son. I feel bad about that, Marie. It was a brief attraction, and she got pregnant. She turned to Orville, who wanted to marry her."

Rodney, always interested in books as gateways to learning, had been instrumental in getting a library in Plentywood and was an active board member. He had hired Alice Young, a quiet girl who loved to read, as a librarian. Rodney, helpful and admiring her abilities as a librarian, charmed her with his attention. She must have been enamored of this intelligent, engaging man to take the risk, and they had a brief affair. Rodney must have been secretly, and briefly, seeing the young librarian when the Salisburys and the Hansens were meeting with *The Producers News* people, Hans Rasmussen and Charlie Taylor. I can easily imagine that awkward, uneasy moment when Alice told him that she was pregnant. Perhaps she waited for him to declare himself, this married man with six children, but he could only give her sympathy and nothing else. In light of her youth and the trouble he had brought into her life, was he ashamed, and embarrassed, and truly sorry? Or was he just relieved when Alice Young, soon after discovering she was pregnant, married Orville Iverson, her boyfriend? That day in Plentywood, as they crossed the street and came face to face with Alice and Stanley, according to my mother, Rodney seemed contrite. Stanley's birthday was June 23, 1927, and Howard Froberg "Budson" Judson Douglas Hansen's birthday was September 4, 1928. These half-siblings were sixteen months apart. It was a prophetic meeting, there on the street in Plentywood, as time was to tell.

When my mother told me this story, she had no ill feelings toward Rodney, nor did she exhibit jealousy. She was just relating the story. He could tell my mother about this affair and she would not judge him, nor would she feel threatened by it. I believe he told her everything, like this unsavory bit of information about his affair with Alice Young. I often thought when I heard these stories as a girl, that Rodney and Marie lived in some sort of emotional isolation from the rest of the world, a bubble of their own creation, with their private language of love and affection. Still, what strength it would take to survive under the small-town scrutiny of Plentywood society.

I imagine it didn't take long for my mother to begin to see she was the one carrying the burden of this philosophy. She was being pummeled by the gossip and disdain of people who had known her since she was a girl. She was the scorned, fallen woman, the seductress, the unfaithful wife, the neglectful mother. Free love was a great idea and made sense to them both, but in experiencing it as a reality, it was impossible to escape the censorship and conventional judgments of a small town and its Christian beliefs. Likely, Rodney could see the injustice for her, and he became open to the idea of marriage. They had had a child together. They began to work tirelessly to make this happen.

Emma, Rodney's wife, was liked and respected in Raymond. She was regarded as hardworking, generous, and a good mother to her six children. She stood by her husband and was, as my sister Camilla told me, rather amused by Rodney's boyish enthusiasms and his ventures into the latest radical idea, but she always supported him. She was also a good friend of Marie's, and the women admired each other and got along well. Emma was a practical, sensible woman and found Marie amusing and fun. They were different, but kindred spirits, too, discussing books, child rearing, recipes. The two families often spent holidays together, with Janis and Jardis babysitting the Hansen kids as the women cooked elaborate meals and laughed in the kitchen. Eventually, the rumors circulated to Emma, for there are always those willing to bring bad news so they can offer sympathy.

When Emma found out, the knowledge that Rodney had been seeing Marie in a clandestine relationship, and that they had a son together, was a huge blow. My sister Camilla recalled her mother's grief and sense of loss and betrayal at this knowledge. Her mother, she said, was like a dazed creature, a ghostly specter, not talking, shuffling from room to room in the early hours of the morning, going about her duties in a vague and distant manner. She quit eating and lost so much weight her clothes hung lifelessly on her shrunken frame.

Whatever was said between Emma and her husband, Rodney, on that fateful day when she told him what she knew, and he verified it, is not a matter of record but rather of conjecture. One can imagine recriminations, hurt, anger, and a remorseful Rodney. He liked his wife and, as a friend, didn't want to hurt her, I'm sure. More telling than anything, though, is that whatever happened between them, he did not give up his "paramour." He continued to see Marie. The community viewed Emma as the victim of her husband and her friend, Marie. As a result, Rodney lost his bid for sheriff in 1928, the year Budson was born. Marie continued living with Andrew, and Rodney still lived with his family. They kept up their outward, respectable lifestyles.

Maybe Emma and Andrew, like so many spouses, were the last to know. Or maybe denial cushioned them from the truth until they were able to handle it. Emma, though, survived this bitter truth and was to outlive them all.

With all the curiosity of a pubescent, moralizing teenager, and assuming my mother would not sleep with two men at the same time, I asked her about this. She said that she told Andrew right away about being in love with Rodney, and that their relationship from then on was that of a brother and sister. Many years later, I had reason to doubt this, but only after her death. At the time, I think she did the right thing by presenting herself to me, her daughter, as an honest woman with integrity. How that matched the reality of their lives in the village of Plentywood, as they kept up appearances by each continuing to live in their family situations, is hard to tell. One can imagine the rumor mill grinding out salacious gossip, only to be confronted by Emma and Rodney together at some event at the Farmer Labor Temple, and Marie, Andrew, and Hans Rasmussen at that same event. Publicly, there were no signs of anger or betrayal in their association. Rodney and Marie continued to be seen together at events too, as they continued to try to convince Andrew and Emma to give them divorces, but to no avail.

All three of the women with whom Rodney fathered children were educated activists for social justice and interesting women. I like to believe, and why not—that he loved my mother best of all. For all the social ostracism she endured being his lover, having his children, I would like that for her. I would also like to believe that my father could be true. More and more as time passed, as they were seen everywhere together, the idea of marriage loomed in importance.

But there were Emma Salisbury and Andrew Hansen, who had to consent to giving these lovers a divorce. Both said no.

To write a meaningful memoir, I have been told, you must have interesting people living in interesting times. Writing this memoir, now, at eighty-five years of age, I feel the drift of time like a lost silent movie. My mother and father did not create interesting times; they were born into them and became a part of that large sweep of humanity that slowly but inexorably moves toward change. Though they undoubtedly created interesting gossip and scandal, there were larger issues that framed the zeitgeist of their time, the scrim that defined their life and purpose. They were not just interested spectators, they were active participants. My father, a member of the Industrial Workers of the World, a Socialist, a Communist, a labor organizer, a farmer, and a man who read widely, was keenly aware of what was happening not only in his locale, but also in the world. He saw a great need for change, for social justice. Capitalism for him, and the many people like him, was a system of exploitation of the worker, with the huge profits going to people who wanted only profits as big as they could get, and cared little or nothing for what happened to those on whom they relied for these profits. He was grounded in that idea, and my mother understood that for him, it was as essential as the experiences that had led him to these conclusions. His fervor was so great, his passion both for her and for the world they lived in coalesced in their relationship. She was open and receptive, and what he said made sense to her. From him, she got the language she needed for her expression of injustice, and she was an eager learner. She carried these beliefs with her until the hour of her death.

All through her life and the choices she made, Marie resonated with the nine-year-old girl in that old photo, standing apart from her family, defiant, vulnerable, alone; but with Rodney, she was more than the sum of her parts. Within his big worldview and his intense devotion, her natural intelligence and imagination found expression. Their dedication to creating a better world for working people through social reform, and their unity of belief, gave them strength in the midst of criticism and disdain. They had each other and a community of friends with similar ideals.

22

In the late 1920s, about the time Budson was born, Rodney and Marie were hearing reports about what was happening in Russia. Most of their information came from the Communist Party USA, headquartered in New York City. The news was often baffling and changeable. Rather than Trotsky being the new leader in Moscow, as they had anticipated, they were hearing reports of intrigue and duplicity. Stalin, the organizational man, had simply outmaneuvered Trotsky, the thinker. Lenin, the head of the government since 1917, had died in 1924, and afterwards Stalin gave Trotsky the wrong date for his funeral so Trotsky missed it. Such are the political ploys that bring down kings. Stalin called Trotsky "Judas Trotsky," and undermined his authority. Even more importantly, Stalin slowly but inexorably stacked the politburo with his comrades, and they had the power. But that wasn't enough. Trotsky was eventually expelled from the USSR in 1929 and assassinated in Mexico in 1940.

Russia under Stalin began a decade of unimaginable repression of its people. The "War in the Countryside," as it was called, which was the collectivization of agriculture, took the lives of 10 million people, half of them from starvation. Purges took the lives of millions more: the intellectuals, university professors, doctors, lawyers, and the peasants who rebelled against Stalin's economic policies. These regular purges terrified people into compliance. The gulags, prisons for dissenters, made them slaves. The revolution that Rodney and Marie and all the radicals and liberals in this country imagined simply evolved into a state as repressive as the one they found in capitalism, only more so. This knowledge must have been a bitter irony for them. Rodney's attachment to the principles of the Russian Revolution was steeped in Marx, Lenin, and Trotsky. With Trotsky banished, stories about Stalin's reign filtered to the most remote outposts, and soon the Plentywood Communists were hearing of Stalin's slaughter of anyone who opposed his views, or might be against the Communist philosophy. The radical element in Plentywood, influenced

by Rodney Salisbury, the Communist sheriff, and Charlie Taylor, editor of
The Producers News, were shocked and astounded by the reality in Mother
Russia. Communist ideals for a more fair and just existence for all workers
was, by Stalin's actions, a bitter betrayal.

The ironies mounted. Rodney and Marie, their friends, and many intellectuals in this country espoused the Marxist-Lenin principles of the
Russian Revolution. Stalin killed or imprisoned the Russian intellectuals
and writers and aimed to control all information. In the United States,
the intellectual revolutionaries were the ones who believed in a world
where reform would be fair to the proletariat; in Russia, such people were
jailed or killed. There was one way to think, and anything else was treason.
Stalin's reign was as brutal as anything seen under the czar, and worse. This
is what the revolution of 1917 came down to.

*You see that book there, on the top shelf? Black with red lettering? That
book was a book your father revered. He often said, and I can hear him as if
he were standing next to me: Marie, that is one of the most important books
in the world. It is an astonishing work by one of the greatest reporters that
ever lived: John Reed. It should be required reading by every student in high
school*—Ten Days That Shook the World.

I was a young girl, maybe ten years old, when this book came into my
consciousness. Sometimes out of curiosity and wanting to know my father,
I would take the book from that top shelf, handle it, and then open it, as
if some secret from my father about this book would be revealed to me.
I would trace his elegant handwriting, "Rodney Salisbury," on the flyleaf.
I would look in the book, read the introduction by Lenin, and leaf through
it, curious about the Russian language I spotted here and there. But I
could not read the whole book. It took a student of history for that, or a
person like my father, whose imagination was fired by the people's revolt,
inspired that they had actually succeeded in overturning the czar. I can
easily imagine that Rodney identified with Reed, had the same passion for
social reform and change. For him, *Ten Days That Shook the World* would
have been a true adventure story that he could identify with. Rodney

would have been twenty-nine during the October revolution. Had he been given the chance, had he been asked, he would have gone with John Reed to Russia. He would have witnessed the revolution, that incredible phenomenon where the people claimed their country and their rights. As it was, he did it vicariously through Reed's experiences in Russia, his writing about it, his friendship with Lenin and Trotsky. As for John Reed, his life had been different from Rodney Salisbury's. Reed grew up in a wealthy neighborhood, went to Harvard, and mingled with T. S. Eliot, Walter Lippmann, and Van Wyck Brooks. But in spirit, they were brothers; they had a parallel vision of a better world through Socialism and Communism. My mother would have loved being a reporter on such an assignment, but she was only sixteen years old when it happened.

Many years later, this same book was made into a film and was in movie theaters in 1981. Warren Beatty was the director and knew this was going to be an expensive film, and because the subject was a positive look at Communism, also hard to finance. In some kind of incredible irony, Beatty was able to convince Charles Bluhdorn, head of Gulf Western (Paramount's parent company) to finance the film.[7] Beatty not only directed the film, but also played the role of John Reed. Diane Keaton was the romantic interest as Louise. I've watched that film many times, but the first time was with a sense of sadness and acute nostalgia. My mother had died a few years before the film's release, but I could just see her, sitting in the audience, leaning eagerly forward as she did when she was totally absorbed. She would have known and recognized so many of the intellectuals of that time who were interviewed by Beatty as the "Witnesses": George Seldes, Roger Baldwin, Henry Miller, Will Durant, to name a few. They were old, and many of them died soon after the film aired. It would have been, in so many ways, a vindication of her life and love for this one man, this revolutionary, and how she had breached convention to be with him. Now, with this movie, people would know and understand—that would have been her hope.

Russia for me is many things, and sometimes I feel as if I have dual citizenship in this country. Bred in Plentywood, hearing endless conversations about the revolution and all things Russian since I was born, I have a psyche steeped in the lore of this vast, cold country. Everything Russian is larger than life, like the novels I read, *War and Peace*, *Anna Karenina*, *The Brothers Karamazov*. It covers a wide expanse of Europe and Asia and is the largest country in our world.

I have been to Russia several times, and the first time I arrived in Finland Station in Leningrad, I thought of Rodney and Marie. It was as if I had entered a Russian novel. In the public square was a statue of Lenin, larger than life. The station was huge, with a high-domed interior, dimly lit. People speaking many languages hurried by to their destinations, most of the men wearing heavy dark coats and fur hats, the women wearing babushkas, dark coats, and sensible shoes.

In Leningrad, there were lines of patient Russians waiting to get food, while familiar American jazz bands were playing on the radio in the stores. There were artists on Nevsky Prospect, circled with people watching them work. The state did not allow any Russian art to be exported or sold. At the time, I was a dedicated European folk dancer, and I was mesmerized by the precise artistry and beauty of professional Russian dancers. There were twelve men and twelve women, all extremely handsome, physically perfect. Right then and there, I decided I would somehow manage to see the Bolshoi next time it came to New York. I kept seeing in my mind's eye the film of Shostakovich's return to Moscow to give a piano recital after a fifty-year absence, and the reception he was given. The Russians support and revere their artists.

23

During the Great War, the farmers in Plentywood had prospered. Rodney, who didn't believe in the war, would have refused to go, but the twins, Janis and Jardis, were born and he was exempted. He was considered more valuable as a farmer, helping the war effort by providing food for the troops and the cities. Ironically for him, it was considered patriotic to farm. Many farmers borrowed money from the banks and bought more machinery to plow more fields, plant more crops and hay for the cattle. It was a boom time, and farmers rode the wave of prosperity.

But after the war, beginning in 1919 and into the next decade, the farmers of Sheridan County witnessed the extremes of weather, with hot summers of over 100 degrees, windblown dust, and parched land. The abundant grasslands were often set on fire by sparks from the engines of the trains that roared through the prairie. The wheat crops were small, and with the grasslands burned from prairie fires, hay for the cattle over the winters was scarce. The wind brought winter storms, and temperatures fell to 30 below and colder, and the cattle were left to fend for themselves. My mother's father raised Longhorns, hardy range animals, but my uncles' forays out into the bleak cold landscape would find them like frozen sculptures, dying from cold and starvation. There was nothing they could do. Marie's weather stories about the high plains were always a hyperbole of disaster, with dead cattle in the winter dotting the barren snow-filled fields, and sparse crops of wheat burned dry by a blazing, indifferent sun. The good weather, abundant crops, and good prices that had marked that one good year in 1918 in Sheridan County, all but disappeared in the following years. Drought left the earth parched and dry. "Black Blizzards" carried the topsoil away and crept under the tightest doors and windows, fatally clogging the lungs of the very young and old. Voracious grasshoppers leveled a field within hours. All these natural disasters created despair and dashed the hopes of even the most stalwart. The 1920s were to see a migration of dejected, worn-out farmers, broke and weary of the struggle, leaving Sheridan County for Texas or Oregon, as Marie's family, the Chapmans, did. Those who stayed and rode it out found it hard to survive. Farmers could barely live on what they produced. It cost more to round up and send the cattle to market than the price they were getting for beef. People were hungry. The stock market crashed in 1929, and year by year, production dwindled. By 1931, Sheridan County experienced complete crop failure. The headlines of *The Producers News* for June 1931 read, "Sheridan County People Face Starvation." The struggle for survival in Plentywood, the fact that people were starving, was a replica of misery all over the United States.

Rodney ran for sheriff in 1928 for the fourth time, but lost the election. This was the same year, in September, that Rodney and Marie's son Budson was born. Sometime during this period, his friend Charlie Taylor told Rodney that his open relationship with Marie Hansen was hurting him politically. Though Rodney and Charlie were good friends, Rodney ignored his warning and continued to see his "paramour," as Charlie called her. By the time the stock market crashed in 1929, the farmers were already experiencing bad times. Rodney was still organizing the farmers; now he was interested in the Farmers Union, another way for farmers to stand together on issues important to agriculture.

Rodney was no longer sheriff and did not have that wage to feed his family. As a farmer and rancher, he was subject to the same perils that afflicted all of his fellow farmers. He had a wife and six children to take care of. By 1933, Prohibition had been repealed, and liquor was flowing freely; there was no lucrative bootlegging black market as a means of livelihood. Emma had a reputation for being resourceful and frugal, and the family cultivated a garden and raised chickens, pigs, and several cows. There was no money. Banks were closed.

C. S. Nelson, the editor who befriended Marie and taught her the newspaper business, trusted friend of her father, Albert Chapman, sold the *Plentywood Herald* to a man named Harry Polk in 1928. This new editor immediately saw himself in total opposition and contrast to *The Producers News*. On the front page of one of the *Herald*'s 1930 issues, a column announcing that Rodney Salisbury was opening The People's Bakery stood next to an adjacent column of an article about Andrew Hansen Flour

Mills providing the flour. Even in these hard times, people brought what wheat they had to Hansen Flour Mills to be ground. The Danish community at Dagmar was struggling but not starving.

The irony did not escape the *Herald*'s readers or the townspeople of Plentywood. By this time, the citizenry must have known about Rodney and Marie's relationship. These articles, and the sly intimations of these front page headlines, were not an accident, and I can imagine the glee, maybe astonishment, that it created in its readers. What is not mentioned is that Marie set up a kitchen serving soup and bread, which she cooked herself. A steady flow of Wobblies, itinerant workers, and hungry people came to her kitchen. She was filling a special need in a dire time, and Rodney helped, as did Andrew with free flour from the mill. They all had an entrepreneurial spirit, particularly in restaurants. I have on my bookshelf a cookbook of Rodney's titled *American Meat Cooking*. On the flyleaf is Rodney's elegant signature, fluid and practiced.

The Producers News had its shenanigans, too. Charles Taylor was no slouch when it came to humorous, sly invective. By 1926, *The Producers News* had swallowed up six local weeklies. His opponents were "small town Kaisers," "patriotic profiteers," "crop grabbers." The *Pioneer Press*, which Taylor called the "*Pie Near*" *Press* and referred to as that "nauseous rag that emits itself once a week from its sty down the street," finally folded. When one of its advertisers, the Elgin Café, run by owner Jim Popescu, pulled its advertising from *The Producers News* because of its Communist leanings, Taylor ran an article saying customers found cockroaches in their soup. Later, to put a fine point on the food at the café, an article appeared in *The Producers News* reporting that a patron pulled a mouse from his stew, and it was generally agreed that Taylor had a plant pull this stunt. I remember my mother making reference to this incident and being amused.

During all of this, Marie Chapman Hansen was aligned with the radical left and its newspaper, *The Producers News*, and with the town's former sheriff, Rodney Salisbury, Plentywood's most well-known and most discussed Communist. Out in Oregon, hearing of their daughter's exploits, her parents were disappointed, angry, and finally turned away from her. She was not to see or hear from them for twenty-five years.

24

Along with the hard times besetting everyone, there were the personal tribulations that affected families in heartbreaking ways—the sickness and death of children; the women who grew old too soon with hard work, unwanted pregnancies, and the lonely life and isolation of the vast plains; the men who were worn and stooped with the endless toil and the futility of hard work, only to be rewarded by the harsh, implacable elements of nature. We don't know all the stories, but we know they have been lived and endured, all the sorrows and griefs of the ages. They are buried there on the high plains of Montana. Rodney and Marie knew something about this firsthand.

Such a tragedy struck the Salisbury family during the heart of the Depression in the spring of 1932. Janis and her twin, Jardis, were lively, playful girls and popular in the township of Raymond, where they were born, as well as in Plentywood, where their father was sheriff. According to their sister Camilla, Janis and Jardis organized something called "The Red Spark Club," which was a Communist youth group that met at the Farmer Labor Temple. They were also the leaders of the Young Pioneers, another Communist youth group, in the Salisbury hometown of Raymond. It was Camilla's opinion that the twins could be difficult and opinionated, especially Janis, having the absolute sense that she was always right. "She made a great revolutionary," Camilla commented wryly. "I remember as a little kid watching her argue religion with one of her schoolmates. She was formidable and could argue you down a rabbit hole."

These youth groups sometimes met for special lessons during school hours, either at the Labor Temple or Brush Lake. The Plentywood school board protested by issuing an edict stating that if students attended these Communist meetings, they could not participate in extracurricular activities. The fight was on, with a response by the Young Communist League denouncing the members of the board as hypocritical. Four girls, including Janis, Jardis, and Emma Taylor, Charlie's daughter, were absent from school one day and attended classes at the Farmer Labor Temple. They all brought excuses, but the teacher refused to accept them, and they were required to stay after school to make up the time. Emma Salisbury entered the fray when Janis was required to stay after school, because unlike the other girls, she had stayed home to help Emma, who was ill. Outraged, she sent Pete Steinov, the Hungarian Wobbly who worked on the Salisbury farm, to get Janis. According to my sister Camilla, Pete wouldn't take "no" for an answer, nor would he listen to what the teacher had to say, and told her to "go to hell." He had been sent on a mission, and he was going to accomplish it. His loyalty to the Salisburys and Hansens was legendary, and in his attempt to rescue Janis a ruckus ensued. Pete Steinov, Camilla recalled, was angry and started yelling. According to the *Plentywood Herald*, the final confrontation with Steinov was at the Salisbury ranch, where the new sheriff, Madsen, had gone to arrest him. High drama ensued. Emma physically and verbally tore into the sheriff to protect Steinov, and the sheriff backed off. Later, Rodney brought Pete into the police station, and he was put on trial. "It was all such a farce," Camilla stated, "and not about the girls being absent, but what they were absent for. It was about politics. The schools carried the capitalist brand of philosophy, and that's what it was about. The verdict came in as guilty, and Pete was fined ten dollars. We all knew why."

After the verdict, according to *The Producers News*, Rodney stood on a table and condemned the whole proceedings, shouting "that the whole case was a fight on the workers and farmers and those working for the overthrow of capitalism; that the school system was a part of the support of capitalism, and the trial was proof of it—there was nothing to the case but a premeditated effort to put a working man in jail."[8]

Rodney saw everything through a radical lens, and he gave no quarter. Yet the value he, Emma, and Marie placed on education was paramount. In some ways, his radicalism was black and white. At the same time, he believed being educated was the highest mark of a civilized human being.

In another comment on public education, in 1933 the Communists supported Hans Rasmussen to run as a school trustee. The curriculum, he proclaimed, rather than concentrating on capitalist leaders and militarism, should also include working-class heroes. Students should have free medical and dental care, as well as free milk.

His bid was rejected, and he received 45 votes to his opponents 316. This was just further evidence that the Communist popularity in Sheridan County was not just waning, but failing.[9]

In the furor of all the political debate, one evening Janis complained of a stomachache and would not eat. Rodney and Emma thought it was just a simple thing and would eventually disappear. And it was true. She seemed to recover for a short time and then became sick again. Later, when she became ill with a fever, nausea, vomiting, chills, and doubled up with pain, they took her to the local physician, Dr. J. C. Storkan. He determined she had appendicitis and performed an operation to remove the diseased appendix, but it was too late. It had burst, and peritonitis had set in. She was fourteen years old, in the local hospital, dying.

While Emma and Janis's brothers and sisters gathered around her, Rodney found Marie, and they went looking for Mike, his oldest son. It was a matter of hours for Janis.

My mother loved all of Rodney and Emma's children, but it was Janis, the Salisbury most interested in her father's worldview, whom she talked about above all the rest.

I've never seen a man more distraught. She was his little revolutionary, lively, and precocious. She used to run up to him, grab his hand, hug him, pull his head down so she could whisper something, and it always made him laugh. She pleased him just by being alive. When she became ill, he thought, with her spirit, she would surely survive. He couldn't imagine it any other way. After the operation, she declined rapidly, until finally he lost hope that she might be saved. He was broken-hearted, weeping. Now we were trying to find Mike, who at seventeen was playing jazz piano wherever a job was offered. He would come home those late nights and keep everyone awake practicing. It was the one thing he had a passion for. Rodney saw it as a dissolute life, though Emma defended him, cherishing this talented son. So he and the piano had moved out of the house. You know, he could never read music, but once he heard a tune, it belonged to him. It was the great jazz age, and Mike had found his true love. We set out to find him, so he could be with his sister in her last hours. We searched the bars, and finally we were told he had gone home, to a room he was renting. When we got there, Mike was in bed, asleep, with two girls. Rodney was disgusted. "Get up," he said, and I've never heard a colder voice. "Your sister is in the hospital, dying. You need to be there. We'll be in the car, waiting."

Janis died that night with her family around her. I wasn't there, of course. We were all grieved, and wondered what kind of memorial service they would have for Janis, not being religious people. A few days later, Rodney called me. "I can't believe she's gone," he said. He sounded sad and tired.

My mother paused here, lost in thought, outlined in sadness as she leaned on the counter and lit a cigarette.

I asked him, "What kind of service, Rodney? What will you do? Something at the Vollmer church, or the Labor Temple?" It was a religious community, you know. Hans Rasmussen had built the Vollmer church on Hansen land in Dagmar. I thought maybe they would choose that place. "We've decided," he said. "At the temple. In the spirit of Janis."

Thinking about all the discussion and controversy about this funeral that has trailed down the years, I imagine how it was that Rodney decided to have this kind of service. It makes sense to me considering what he believed, and how for him, belief turned into direct action, the Greek idea of praxis. My father was never more sincere and aware than when he decided on this funeral. He did not pause to consider what the controversy might be between his thinking and the religious community of Lutherans and Catholics in the area. He was thinking of his daughter, and who she was.

Janis Salisbury died on Tuesday, March 1, 1932. The following Saturday her funeral was held at the Farmer Labor Temple, standing room only. The temple was redolent with the many flowers that were sent by the local farmers, *The Producers News*, the United Farmers League, the Young Pioneers, Janis's classmates, and the Communist Party USA. The coffin was covered with flowers, and over it was placed a red flag. Red and black draperies covered the windows, which were emblazoned with hammer and sickle symbols. The people attending rose and together sang "The International": "The workers flag is deepest red / it flies above our martyred dead." Hans Rasmussen officiated, and gave a touching speech about the loss of this young comrade and her importance in the community, and Eric Bert, now editor of *The Producers News*, talked about Janis's devotion as a dedicated Bolshevik. Charlie Taylor also spoke, remarking on her dedication to the cause. The Salisbury family, according to Camilla, all sang and danced during the memorial service. Jardis, Janis's twin, and oldest brother, Mike, played the piano, and Rodney danced a jig. Not once during the service were there any references to God or Jesus mentioned. The religious community of Plentywood was offended, and this funeral formed an even more defined split in the Plentywood community.

Later that same day, Janis was buried at the Salisbury farm. As her coffin was lowered, Rodney recited the following poem he had written in her honor.

You Fought a Fight

You fought a fight, a long good fight
Is all that we can say;
Sleep on, sleep on, your work is done,
Brave fighter for the day.
Kind mother earth who gave you birth
Receives you to her breast.
For us the fight, for you the night.
The night of well-earned rest.
Sleep on, sleep on, your work is done.
Sleep on, sleep on, sleep on . . .

Rodney never got over her death, and was a man often silent in mourning for this wild, simpatico daughter.

25

Many people believe this Bolshevik funeral was the undoing of Rodney's political career. The "Mainstreeters," businessmen, bankers, lawyers, and town folks represented by the *Plentywood Herald* were outraged at this funeral, the godless tribute to a political ideal rather than a supreme deity. One can imagine how the Bolshevik funeral, and the relationship of Rodney Salisbury and Marie Hansen, offended these conventional citizens.

Many years later, old enough to collect Social Security, Camilla and I visited Plentywood. In talking with old-timers, it was one of the first things they mentioned: the godless Bolshevik funeral. One woman announced that her parents did not let her go, and totally disapproved. At this, Camilla took umbrage, becoming grim and tight-lipped, and abruptly left the room. Janis's funeral had become a part of their collective memory, and people were quick to tell us how she was still buried on the old Salisbury farm. No amount of factual evidence could dispel this myth. In truth, Janis had been exhumed from the old Salisbury farm and moved with the family to Missoula, circa 1936, and was buried in the Missoula cemetery. Later, she would be joined there by her father.

In an odd twist of fate, I saw her tombstone recently in the most unlikely of circumstances. Rick and Debbie Orosco once lived in Plentywood on the same property that belonged to Rodney Salisbury. Now, they live on our family farm at Arlee, Montana, the farm I inherited from my mother, Marie Chapman Hansen. The Oroscos know all of the history of the Bolshevik funeral and the myth of Janis's burial. Visiting the graveyard in Missoula on Memorial Day, they saw that Janis's tombstone was cracked and broken. They secreted it away, and brought it home to repair. "There were carnations on her coffin," Rick said, showing me a carnation in glass. "We'll put it back together, and put these glass beads around it for decoration."

I thanked them for taking care of the sister I had never known. We were a little weepy. We hugged.

During that same year that Janis died in March and the Bolshevik funeral took place to honor her, Rodney Salisbury ran for governor of Montana on the Communist ticket. He announced his candidacy in the early summer, and he was nominated at the Communist convention in Great Falls, August 1932. He also had the backing of the Communist Party USA. One would guess that he understood something about the political and personal climate that was growing around him. By this time, it was general knowledge that he was having an affair with a married woman, and had even fathered a child with her. The courthouse robbery, considered an inside job, cast suspicion on him, though he was exonerated in a deposition held by the insurance company. And surely he knew the political climate was changing in Sheridan County. Yet against these almost insurmountable odds, he ran for governor of the state of Montana. Communism in the county was breaking down and meeting ever more resistance by the townspeople. The "Mainstreeters" in Plentywood, fearing the Communists, formed an organization of both Republicans and Democrats, calling themselves the Taxpayers Economy League.[10] One can imagine the firm resolve, on ideological grounds, of these citizens to rid themselves of the Communists. While the Nonpartisan League had been open in its Communist affiliation, as had the Farmer Labor Party, the United Farmers League was more blatant in its connection with the Communist Party USA. By 1932, the Farmer Labor Party was gone, and had been supplanted by the openly Communist United Farmers League. Rodney Salisbury was, as was known at the time of Janis's funeral, the secretary of that organization.

There was always in Sheridan County the changing political scene, and sometimes it played out like a soap opera. Rodney and Charlie Taylor were a vital part of it all. Because of the work of *The Producers News*, the Communist Party in New York and Moscow became interested in Charlie Taylor. His recognition and favor within the party made him somewhat of a celebrity, but it also weakened the radical movement in Sheridan County. His voice, through the paper, with its energy, focused radicalism and withering humor toward those who disagreed with him, and had kept the farmers interested and talking. Without his consistent voice directly cheering them on, educating them to what was fair for them, they flagged. The necessary tools of organizing, getting out the paper, and being a consistent voice for the farmers was weakening under the various editors that took Charlie's place when he was gone.[11] At one time, he was invited by the secretary of the Communist Party in New York to attend the International Anti-Imperialist League conference in Paris, but true to his nature, Charlie Taylor had too many irons in the fire. He was not always on his home ground in Plentywood, either. He pursued his interest in radium, spent time in his hometown of Koochich County, Minnesota, working in lumber mills, and lectured for the Communist Party USA around the country. He couldn't attend the Paris conference, though he understood the honor.

By 1928, Taylor had fallen out with the Russian Communist Party because he supported Leon Trotsky, as did Rodney. In fact, Trotskyites in the United States were expelled from the party. That same year, Mother Bloor, representing the Communist Party of Russia, came to Plentywood and at the Farmer Labor Temple denounced "Taylor, Salisbury, and their ilk" as not supporting the revolution.[12]

My mother, speaking of "Mother Bloor" years later, often laughed when she recalled how Bloor flirted and seduced young handsome men in town. She had the eye for Mike Salisbury, Rodney's handsome oldest son. How successful she was is not a matter of record.

Rodney had lost his last bid for sheriff in 1928 and probably understood the reasons, such as the scandal about the courthouse robbery, which had never been solved, and his blatant affair with Marie Hansen, a married woman. Finally, though, it was the Bolshevik funeral and its godless tribute to a young Communist pioneer that had the whole town talking. The religious roots went deep, especially the Lutheran church of the Danish and Scandinavian communities. Dagmar was liberal, as part of their tradition, but it had been established as a religious community. The more spread out the county became, the more Lutheran churches were built to accommodate those living farther away. The Catholics, Methodists, and Evangelicals were represented, too. Those "Mainstreeters," such as the Catholics and the Lutherans, the businessmen and bankers, had firm roots in their Christian beliefs. A committee of these citizens in the late 1920s and early 1930s met the newly hired teachers each autumn at the train station in Plentywood. They were informed that as a part of their employment they were to be good models for the children. This meant they were to lead exemplary lives and definitely have nothing to do with the "Reds" or attend any of the meetings, dances, or celebrations that went on in a continual stream in the Farmer Labor Temple with its red flags, and hammer and sickle banners.[13] Many of their students attended the Bolshevik funeral, but it was verboten for the teachers. The line was drawn.

The *Plentywood Herald* and its editor, Harry Polk, set out to get rid of the "Reds" once and for all. Both newspapers had a running, contentious battle for the minds and loyalties of the Sheridan County citizenry. The united front of the Republicans and Democrats in a "fusion" ticket was remarkable in that they had understood their strength was in their cohesiveness against the Communists. It was in the best spirit of Charlie Taylor in its tactical correctness, and it paid off.

Considering every obstacle that was in Rodney's path as he ran for governor, I try to understand why he did. I hazard it has something to do with his complex character, his charismatic personality. He wasn't going to give up without a fight, even though the odds were stacked against his winning. It's conceivable that he ran because he had lived his whole life in engagement with various organizations that he envisioned as helping the oppressed in the capitalist system. Perhaps the recent death of his daughter, Janis, was a compelling reason, too. And there were supporters, people rallying around him, giving him the good words that meant so much to him. Charlie Taylor ran for senator at the same time, and once again warned Rodney that his affair with his "paramour" would be damaging to his political aspirations. According to my mother, he was encouraged by the support he had, and thought it outweighed the resistance of the "Mainstreeters."

He was popular, and people liked to be around him, drinking hootch, smoking cigars, talking politics. It was his life's blood, you know. Charlie warned him that I was holding him back, and they had a terrible quarrel. It almost ended their friendship. Of course, Emma Salisbury had a lot to say about this, too. But there were those old friends, old loyal party members, and he was sure they would be there for him. I wasn't so sure, though, you know; I knew something about loss of friendship, certain betrayals, small-mindedness. He did too, but ignored it.

26

Rodney Salisbury's ideals were ingrained. What he saw, surely, was a need. The Depression times were such that he could see the despair and wanted to leap into the fray and help. All he had to do was look around him to see the poverty, the helpless farmers, the hungry children. Considering the political climate, and the facts and innuendos that were so much the skin of his reputation, I wonder if running for governor wasn't for him a last hurrah.

Though Charlie Taylor had many times warned Rodney that his affair with Marie Hansen was harming him politically and cautioned him not to be so overt in his attention to her, Rodney never left her or quit seeing her. I believe Charlie Taylor was right, though, in recognizing that this affair was ruining Rodney's political chances, but still Rodney made the choice. He understood, I'm sure, that had Marie never happened in his life, his path politically would have been different, more successful. In all her stories, they were always together, always trying to get their spouses to give them a divorce. I try to imagine what it was like for them, how they were managing to continue on in the midst of so much ridicule and loss. By this time, they had been together about seven years. Marriage didn't look too possible, but they never lost hope. They wanted to be recognized as a committed couple. They faced the future optimistically.

The Producers News headline on Friday, November 2, 1932, read VOTE COMMUNIST TUESDAY NOV. 8. In that same paper, on the front page, was a picture of Rodney Salisbury running for governor of the state of Montana. The article is glowing in its praise of him. He is a "well-known person for help." He is a "friend and advisor." "State of Montana could not find a better man for that office." Another headline read, ONLY THE COMMUNIST PARTY OPPOSES WAR. There was also notice that there would be a "final Red Campaign Rally" at the Farmer Labor Temple. Charlie Taylor always understood that getting people together at their very own Farmer Labor Temple for food, music, dancing, and speakers drew a crowd. Folks came from Dagmar, Raymond, Scobey, Plentywood, and

Outlook. (Did any of those teachers, forewarned about attending events at the Farmer Labor Temple, feel they were missing out? There was such revelry there, and it included many of the parents of children they taught.) It was promised Charlie Taylor would speak, along with others. I'm sure that Rodney Salisbury was there, as well as his wife, Emma, and Marie with her husband, Andrew Hansen. This was not one of my mother's stories. She just casually mentioned, when she spoke of Rodney running for governor, that *both families were there to support him and cheer him on. It was a good time. Emma, of course, and Mother Bloor were with him on the campaign trail.*

I'd come to recognize that noncommittal look, the steadiness of love and grief, her lot in life.

The *Plentywood Herald* staunchly backed the fusion ticket of the Taxpayers Economy League. In an article before the election, the editor impassioned darkly, "Communism in Sheridan County means even more than endorsement of the overthrowing of our national government. It means the return to power in this county of Charles E. Taylor and Rodney Salisbury. If any of the candidates on the communist ticket should be elected, no one questions they will be under the absolute control of these two men."[14] What strikes me here is the fear tactic, and the perception that these two men wielded such power that they must be contained. Their power and rule means "even more than the overthrow of the government." It's hyperbole and fear mongering at its best, and as the results were to show, it worked.

His opponent for governor in the race in 1932 must have been daunting for Rodney. The popular incumbent, John E. Erickson, was running on the Democratic ticket, and in a close race, he won over the opposing Republican, Frank E. Hazelbaker, 104,949 to 101,105. The candidate for the Socialist Party was a man named Christian Yegan, and he garnered 6,317 votes. Rodney Salisbury, the Communist candidate, received 2,008 votes, only 6 votes more than the Liberty candidate William R. Duncan. It was a stunning defeat, punctuated by the fact that Rodney had not even taken Sheridan County. Camilla was later of the opinion that he should have run as a Democrat, and even hinted that Rodney had some regret that he didn't.

27

That same year, Franklin Roosevelt was elected president and ushered in the New Deal. Also, as luck and the weather would have it, 1933 was a good year for farmers, and wheat prices were up as the drought of previous years relented. Adding to this, Roosevelt's New Deal programs were helping the Plentywood farmers, and they were riding the wave of government-generated prosperity. Farmers were getting some subsidies, unemployed and unmarried men were getting jobs with the Civilian Conservation Corps, and the current Plentywood courthouse was built with funds from the Works Progress Administration. The radicals' previous ideals about a commonwealth, where the cost of production would enter into the price for goods, was now realized in government assistance programs. Survival was the goal. The farmers were worn and weary of the struggle, and Roosevelt was helping. It wasn't the revolution, but it was real, in the present, and it offered relief. According to the records, from March 1933 until 1939, Montana received $389 million in federal relief funds, and an additional $142 million in loans.[15] Rodney believed that the farmers' organizations he had backed, especially the Farm-Holiday Association of which he was local president, had been effective in determining this outcome by getting the government's attention focused on the farmers and their plight. All of this weakened the radical movement in Sheridan County, though the stalwarts hung on, fighting for the old dream, missing the camaraderie of those exciting times. The arguments between the Stalinists and Trotskyites were still echoing across Sheridan County, but getting fainter and fainter.

Still the Depression dragged on, despite the intervention of the government and Roosevelt's policies. It was the beginning of government assistance programs and brought about Social Security, a program offering economic security for the elderly, one of the lasting benefits of the Roosevelt era.

The Christmas of 1932 was a hard time for the Hansen and Salisbury families, and especially so for Rodney and Marie. They were witness to the hardship all around them, and felt it personally in their own lives. In the past, when the Salisburys and the Hansens were friends, they would have spent Christmas together and attended the New Year's dance at the Farmer Labor Temple. But those days were gone forever. Before they parted to spend the holidays with their families, Rodney promised to once again ask Emma for a divorce, and Marie was going to implore Andrew to let her go, too.

Free love and the contempt of her friends was wearing Marie down. She was desperate to marry Rodney, and he was trying to persuade Emma to do the right thing, but she was not interested. He was persuasive, but she had nothing to gain by letting him have a divorce. Marie was the enemy, and Emma expressed her bitterness toward my mother, whom she considered the cause of Rodney's estrangement and the breakup of her family. This was one way she could punish both of them. She held the power, and heartbroken though she was, she used it to punish them. Understandably, after learning of their relationship, she never spoke to Marie again.

Andrew's refusal to divorce Marie, thus allowing her to marry the father of the son he was raising as his own, is puzzling. Did he, after all she had said and done, still love her? Or did he, in some intuitive way, know that Rodney would never get a divorce from Emma? The couples were once friends, and it would not be surprising if Emma and Andrew discussed the situation, maybe even commiserated with each other. Andrew's actions through this time, up until he finally granted the divorce, seemed based on something he understood about Rodney and Marie that Marie didn't. One thing he did know was that, obviously, Rodney was married and had six children. Maybe that fact alone led him to believe that Emma would never grant him a divorce, and that Marie and Rodney would never marry.

As the story played out, this is, for me, the greatest puzzle. As I sit here this somber autumn afternoon, going back into the archives of time, there are many questions and uncertainties that assail me. Andrew Hansen is the most profound mystery of all.

That afternoon, we met at The Producers News. *Andrew and his father, Jens, were at the mill fixing something with the motor. There was no money to buy parts, so they had to figure out the problem. We needed the mill to be working. Times were so bad, and we served a wide area of farmers. They were worried, and Andrew was short-tempered. Jimmy was just a boy, but he wanted to go with them and help, but Andrew was scornful. "You think you can help?" And he gave that little snort of contempt. Jimmy was crushed. Moments like that, I'll tell you Pet, I hated and despised Andrew Hansen.*

She paused, back in that tumultuous time. She lit a cigarette, absorbed in her reflections. I was about to get up and walk away when she continued:

I walked from our house to the News *office in thirty-below weather. It was an early winter storm, you can't imagine the cold, Jode. Congealed the spine, you know. When I walked in the office, there was Rodney standing by the stove, and when he looked at me, he smiled that eager, big smile of his. But he was looking worn and tired, pale. He had a way of just wordlessly taking me in his arms, holding me for the longest time. I knew he would not be happy with my news. It was late January, and knowing the rhythms of my body, I was pretty sure. We had not seen each other for several days. "I'm going to ask Andrew again for a divorce," I said. "Oh, God, Marie . . . how can we do this? Emma keeps saying no. 'You have these children, and after all, you need to support them, Rod.' It's true, Marie. As if I weren't doing enough. Truth is, I don't know what more I can do."*

We just looked at each other. The times were hard, money was scarce. How could I say what I had to say? I had a friend who had gotten herself out of a pregnancy; could I do that?

In my mind's eye, I can see her in the kitchen at Arlee, leaning on the table, hung over, shaking, a full cup of coffee handy, and always smoking. Her storytelling came out of melancholy, a sense of desperate loss. This particular story was an important one for her, and it was repeated with small variation, drinking or sober, in the early years of my life.

She told Rodney, on this occasion, late December of 1932 or January of the next year, 1933, that she was pregnant. What he said to her came out of love and compassion for her; he was also remembering that other girl who had died less than a year before—his Janis. He said to my mother, "Let it be a girl."

The five years between my brother Budson and myself was the longest time my mother had between five pregnancies. She was often lonesome, being the brunt of so much criticism, and she missed her family. Sometime during this pregnancy, she and Rodney visited her brother, Colie, in Wyoming. He was the only contact she had with her eight other siblings, all of whom were living in Oregon. There is a picture taken of them during this visit: my mother, father, Uncle Colie, his oldest daughter Ruby, and a neighbor. My mother looks a little tentative, thin-faced, vulnerable, a look I recognize. To me, Rodney appears confident, strong, a powerful, protective presence. He understands the politics of gender: the choices they have made are harder for her than for him.

She dreaded being pregnant—the morning sickness, the nausea, the birthing. After five years of avoiding it, she was pregnant again. She was small and narrow hipped, and giving birth was always a long, painful process for her. She heard that there was a doctor in Minot, North Dakota, who advertised a special, painless childbirth experience called the "Twilight Sleep." It would have been reasonable that Rodney often traveled to North Dakota, for his mother still lived there, and under the guise of visiting her, he could be with Marie. I know from her stories that he was there with her most of the time during the final month of her pregnancy.

Curious as to what this miracle birthing process was, I discovered "Twilight Sleep" is the translation of the German word *Dammerschlaf*. It involves an injection of morphine and scopolamine to produce an amnesic state; the patient is awake, but doesn't remember the ordeal or pain of childbirth. Sometimes, the drugs can cross the placenta and enter the baby, affecting its nervous system. When we see a baby slapped on its bottom, that's to make sure it wakes up, and this practice was begun with the "Twilight Sleep."

Marie and Rodney went to Minot, and stayed there the month before delivery, until the baby was born. My brother Jim swears that our mother made up the whole story about the "Twilight Sleep," that it was a ruse so she and Rodney could be together at the birth of this girl child. The venture was financed with money from Andrew. For whatever reason, she did not have the "Twilight Sleep." She was in labor for eight hours, and I was taken with forceps, and arrived with a broken arm and a small scar by my right eye. At any rate, Andrew sent her money while she was there, and would have understood her fear of childbirth, having experienced her struggles with their first child, Jim. Many years later, long after they were divorced, my brother Jim related that the cancelled checks that Andrew sent Marie at this time, dated July and August of 1933, were still in the safe in the mill at Wolf Point, transferred there from Plentywood. Why Andrew kept them is a puzzle. The actions of Andrew Hansen are, for me, fraught with mystery. He always had a special place in his heart for his non-son, Howard Froberg "Budson" Judson Douglas Hansen. Many years later when Budson joined the Navy at seventeen, he was told: "You can't have this many names. Choose the name you prefer." He chose the name that was Andrew's Danish legacy, Howard Froberg. Froberg was Andrew's mother's maiden name.

Marie returned from Minot with the new baby, Jo Anne Adaire, born August 19, 1933, and brought her to the Plentywood house where Andrew and her other three children—Jim, nine, Anneva, seven, and Budson, five—were living. Rodney and Marie, together now for seven years, were still mainly housed with their married spouses, but this was for appearances only. They were seen everywhere together and were openly affectionate with each other. When Rodney walked through the door of his home to Emma and his six children, he was just the dad returning from another one of his journeys on the organizing trail. Marie returned home to her own children, two of whom were fathered by a man other than her husband. One can imagine how difficult this charade of respectability must have been for her. Aside from Rodney and a few old friends, she had little support, and she was the brunt of more and more criticism. She had not heard from her parents for years. Across the miles from eastern Montana to Oregon, she could feel her mother's withering contempt; from her father, his sorrow and disappointment in her.

Free love was exciting when it carried the passion of new love, but it was now more and more a burden. Returning from their journeys together, Rodney and Marie always had to go their separate ways and return home to their spouses. They had nowhere else to go.

Soon after her arrival from Minot with her baby girl, Marie received some stunning news: Andrew informed her that they were leaving Plentywood, and his brother, Ted, was going to take over the Plentywood mill. Andrew was moving the family to Wolf Point, and he would take over the mill there, which he owned. At this unsuspected news, Marie was desperate. She and Rodney would be separated, and what could they do? What I've gleaned and been able to piece together from my mother, and from others along the way, is that Andrew's family, his father, brothers, sisters, aunts, and uncles—those stalwarts of the Danish community at Dagmar—were stepping into the debacle. They were going to act on behalf of Andrew Hansen, and see if separating Marie and Rodney might save this marriage. They believed in changing the geography, rather than breaking up the family unit, such as it was. Why Andrew was still saying no to a divorce is a puzzle, since he, unlike Rodney, had reasons that would guarantee him one in a court of law. At the root of it all, I think, it had to do with Danish values pertaining to loyalty and marriage vows. People were not perfect; still, family and tradition were relevant, and they were the boundaries, the cultural glue, that kept society from crumbling into chaos. Now there were four children in his household, two that were clearly not his own: Budson, five years old, and the new baby girl, Jo Anne. What the machinations were behind the scenes, the conversations, the deliberations and speculations, one can only guess. Emma Salisbury was a part of it all, too, trying to salvage what could be saved of her family life. Marie, meanwhile, was prevailing upon Andrew for a divorce, and Rodney was trying to get Emma to agree to a divorce, too.

Marie was helpless. She had to go with Andrew and her children, but according to my brother Jim, she was seldom home. Her housekeeper, Mrs. McCauley, took care of the children while Andrew worked. Marie came and went. My sister Anneva had a long and affectionate daughter-like relationship with Mrs. McCauley until the woman died. Leora Wine, Mrs. McCauley's daughter, was often at the house and also took care of the children. She and her mother thought Marie Hansen was negligent of her children, and they felt righteous in their ongoing gossip about her. They were sympathetic to Andrew and his plight, and talked about how derelict Marie was, how neglected he and his children were. When Andrew's sisters visited from Dagmar, Mrs. McCauley and Leora took every opportunity to let them know how bad the situation was, and how they were saving the day by taking care of the children and the house during Marie's regular absences.

I'm sure my mother, when she returned to the Wolf Point house, was too distracted to notice much, at least in the beginning. On one of her returns to the house, she realized that Leora Wine was a regular presence at the house, even more than Mrs. McCauley, whom she had hired.

Knowing Andrew, it didn't take great wisdom to figure out what was happening. He had an invitation, and he took it. Let's just say I wasn't surprised.

The story, though, repeated so often it became a mantra of my youth, was that Emma would give them a carrot of promise that she would divorce Rodney if they could get the necessary money for college, or for a car, or for dental work, an endless list. Then, with the money in hand, she would have yet another reason, or excuse, why she would not give the divorce.

Rodney would go to her, plead with her to let him go, and she was always calm, and he would get angry out of frustration, and come back to me defeated, once again. She would tell him that he needed to care for his children, and that if he could get a certain amount of money, she would let him go, get a divorce. That's what she started doing. So we'd do everything we could. I would get money from Andrew's account, Rodney would work, and he'd take the money to her, and she would say yes, but—what about college, we must think about that, Rod. And so it went.

Marie, meanwhile, was angrily persisting in her efforts to get a divorce from Andrew. As days passed, their time together was fraught with quarrels and accusations, pleading and tears, but he would not yield. Marie, in her desperation, threw the truth at him, trying to convince him to divorce her. I think he wanted to protect her, and intuited that Emma Salisbury would never relent, and Marie and Rodney would never marry. Again, perhaps it is all quite simple: He loved his wife, and he liked the children.

Years later, the summer I was turning eighteen years old and living with my mother in Arlee, my brother Jim brought me the news that "the old man" as he called Andrew, wanted to see me. I went to my mother and told her, thinking she would refuse, and she did hesitate. Then Jim said, "Her sister Anneva wants to see her too," and our mother agreed.

Jim and I traveled those long, lonesome miles from Missoula to Wolf Point over washboard roads through prairie country and fields of wheat disappearing into the horizon. We arrived so early in the morning that the house was dark. "It is the same house," Jim reminded me, "where our mother lived briefly when you were a baby." We waited in the car, and then the kitchen light came on, and this man was sitting at a table by the window. I waved, and he waved back. When we entered the house, he had tears in his eyes. "You look like your mother," he said when I hugged him. Then, "See those two little hooks above the door? Your swing hung there when you were a baby."

Marie and Rodney made an interesting visit to Williston, North Dakota, looking for a solution to their married state. They were searching for a home. In the archives I have been keeping these many years relating to my parents, I have a letter. Where this letter came from, who the writer of the letter was, I have no idea. I just know it contains some interesting information about Rodney Salisbury and Marie Hansen. The letter is dated March 20, 1934, from Williston, North Dakota. The writer of the letter is addressing the letter to a man called "Bud," obviously a relative or good friend. They own some land they want to sell, because they are in debt and owe taxes, and a Mrs. Hansen has expressed interest in ten acres by the river. The writer says: "Then—and more important—came a visit last week from Mrs. Hansen, of Plentywood, who wants to buy 10 acres of land down by the river and build a fine house there. She wants to get her children out of the town and wants to get somewhere where there are trees and the possibility for irrigation. Mr. Salisbury brought her down. Of course I have known her for many years as she is one of the old Socialists there and her husband runs the flour mill."

When Rodney and Marie made this visit, they were obviously contemplating a place of their own. Budson was almost six, and Jo Anne was seven months old.

What they wanted was to be able to live together, but it seemed more doubtful all the time. The times were hard, money was scarce. How could they buy land and build a house? Rodney had six children to take care of. Andrew was being responsible for not only his own two children, but Rodney and Marie's Budson and Jo Anne.

As an aside, I am reminded that my grandmother Salisbury lived in North Dakota, and according to Camilla, Rodney was a regular visitor to see his mother. When she heard the rumors about his affair with a married woman, she firmly admonished him. She was a great defender of his wife, Emma, whom she liked and admired. My mother did meet her on one of the trips to North Dakota, but there was no story. In fact, my mother was curiously silent about Rodney's mother. I did ask her once about my grandmother, and she said, as I remember, in an offhand manner, *I think she was an Irish washerwoman, or something.* Her face had that flat, non-committal look. It struck me, even as young as I was at the time, that it was a romantic cliché, captured for the moment. I don't remember how old I was, but I know I thought this was funny, and wanted to laugh. An Irish washerwoman, really?

*Maggie and Albert Chapman with their children in a wheat field
in Plentywood, Montana, circa 1910. Marie is in front, to the left.*

*The Chapman girls, dressed beautifully by
Maggie. Back row, left to right: Marie, Grace,
front row, left to right: Ann, Eva (Billy).*

*Cec and Coleman in France in World War I, 1918,
both were decorated war heroes.*

Left to right, Colie's daughter Ruby, Marie, Gwen's father, Colie's wife Gwen, Rodney, Colie.

Maggie Chapman wearing silk and lace; she was always immaculate when she went out.

Beautiful, stylish Aunt Grace.

Marie after she learned to drive.

*Marie Chapman as a stylish young flapper after she returned
to Plentywood from St. Catherine's Academy in St. Paul, Minnesota.*

Andrew and Marie, c. 1924. In the Navy, Andrew played in the Sousa band.

Marie and her firstborn, Jim.

Anneva and Jim, July 2, 1928.

Rodney Russell Salisbury as a young man.

Farmer Labor Temple, built by the citizens of Plentywood in 1924,
was a popular venue for social and political events.

This is the Jean Jacque Henner painting Rodney gave to Marie at the birth of Budson (Howard).

Jim always loved animals; here he is with a cat buddy.

Joe and Ada in front of the Billings house.

Rodney Salisbury, age forty-six, 1933, in the photo he used when he ran for governor that year.

Rodney Salisbury's grave marker, Missoula, Montana. Note that the stone carver misspelled his name.

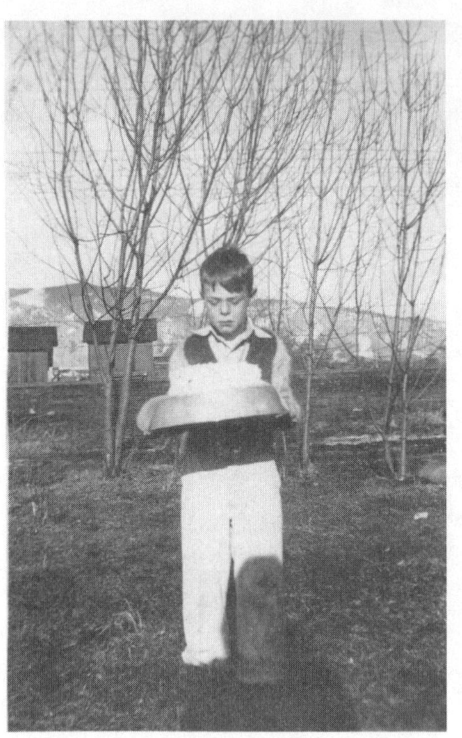

*Edward Lawler, benefactor
of Marie and her children.*

*Roger's eighth birthday, the one and only
time that one of Marie's children with
Rodney had a party with a cake.*

Marie with a fine feathered friend.

Jo Anne, just six, in the garden at Billings.

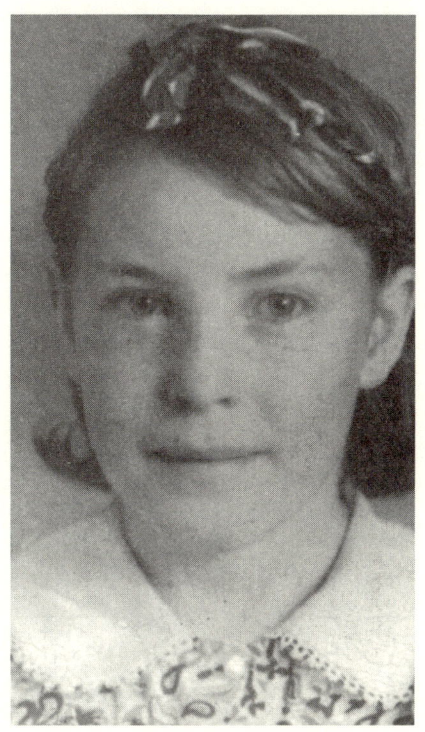

Jo Anne, age eight.

Roger on Buck.

Jim at seventeen just before he joined the Navy.

Jim and Andrew, Jim on leave from Navy.

Mike Salisbury at Arlee.

Grandma and Grandpa Chapman late in their lives.

Roger in Navy bootcamp.

Budson and Stanley together in Arlee on Stanley's eighteenth birthday.

Budson (Howard) as the editor in chief of his college newspaper.

*Wedding picture 1952, back row: Howard, Roger, Jo Anne, Anneva, Anneva's husband Ed;
front row: Barbara, her father, mother, sister, and husband.*

Jo Anne when she was a teacher, 1962.

Marie and Anneva.

Three generations enjoying California sunshine, top to bottom: Jo Anne, Marie, and Allison.

Roger, Marie, Allison, and Keith.

Reunion 1981 of Stanley, Jim, Jo Anne, and Budson.

Mike Salisbury, Rodney's first son, jazz musician.

Stanley in Seattle, about age fifty.

Eugene, Rodney's second son.

*Vern, Allison, and Jo Anne Troxel
in Bozeman, Montana.*

Jo Anne, Camilla, and Allison.

131

Sometime in 1932, Rodney organized the Farm Holiday Association, sprouted as an action arm of the Farmers Union, an organization that had roots in the Midwest and Plains area. This group was active for just a few years, 1932 to 1937, and *The Producers News* supported it. It was essentially a grassroots organization that supported farmers, and encouraged them to withhold their produce, take a "holiday" from production, and even destroy their crops until cost of production was realized. They marched on capitals, made headlines pressuring state and local governments at all levels, and were "unquestionably the most important organization of the farm revolt of the 1930s."[16]

To try to speak coherently in linear time of the complex issues of the farm revolt of the 1930s is a herculean task. Trying to assess the sum total of Rodney's activism, one thing becomes clear to me. He was a farmer and grassroots organizer who knew the perils of farming in eastern Montana and the Dakotas, a man of the land. As organizations merged and were subsumed by others, or sprouted up, he would alternate from one organization to another in order to be a part of the farm revolt, a revolt that centered on getting a fair price for produce, reasonable railroad fares to ship wheat, and avoiding foreclosure by the banks.

In his relatively brief life, Rodney was a man of many parts, all merging in one seamless whole. He was a Socialist, a member of the Communist-based Nonpartisan League and the IWW, secretary to the United Farmers League, a union man, and an activist with the National Farm Holiday Association, where he held the local office of president until he died. Viewing it from a vantage point of these many years later, I see my father always as a man responding to circumstances around him, having a larger vision beyond the limits of any party affiliation. Why one group melted into another, or another radical group emerged, and then another, has to do with factions, disagreements, arguments, inconsistencies—much of it from the Communist Party USA. Many local people disliked the autocratic Communist Party of New York telling them what to do locally. Rodney was essentially a grassroots organizer, and philosophically, a follower of Trotsky and Lenin. During the Russian Revolution, Trotsky and Stalin were in agreement as Bolshevik-Leninist comrades. They became enemies in the 1920s and disagreed about each other's form of Leninism. Trotsky was critical of Stalin for suppressing democracy and not having an economic plan for the future. Trotsky, like Lenin, believed in the theory of "permanent revolution" where Russia would become the model for revolution in other feudal and capitalistic regimes, while Stalin's vision was limited to Russia. Both Charlie and Rodney held the view of Trotsky, and when the news trickled down about Stalin's atrocities and the banishment of Trotsky, Rodney went rogue.

It was this last organization, the Farm Holiday Association, that lost him his friendship with Charlie Taylor. Taylor and Rodney had been friends since 1918 when the United Farmers League had sent Charlie to take over *The Producers News*. Both men had been important and familiar figures in the Plentywood radical farm movement, and their families were close. They were a mutual admiration society, with Rodney enjoying Charlie's rapier, sophisticated wit, and Charlie admiring Rodney's unshakeable stance for economic justice, his intelligence, and his quick laughter. They had even conspired together about a possible cure for cancer. They were bonded by political camaraderie, and both were Trotskyites. Charlie, though, by getting the attention of the Communist Party USA, was often gone from Plentywood, lecturing around the country for the United Farmers League.

I am not sure why the Farm Holiday Association was such a threat to the "revolution" unless it was taking Rodney's focus to another group, rather than maintaining solidarity with the prescribed Communist doctrine and the United Farmers League. This was the same party that had backed him in running for governor of Montana. There is something about all this squabbling and jockeying for position that seems like a bunch of churlish boys, rather than serious people fighting for world justice. One accusation stated that the Farm Holiday Association was a tool of the capitalist system, another that Rodney was "being a traitor to the revolution," and again that he was a "counter-revolutionary."[17] Given Rodney's activist history, his engagement in the Farm Holiday Association was not unusual, as his actions to help the farmer were grounded in the local situation that he knew and had ties with.

Charlie Taylor, in what I would describe as a fawning gesture (he'd had his outs with the party, too), currying favor with the party, agreed that Rodney should be "ousted." Charlie wrote a guest editorial from Nebraska, where he was organizing for the Communist Party USA. He sent it to *The Producers News*, which during his absence from Plentywood was under the editorship of Wallace. In this letter he stated that his "life long friend," through his work with the Farm Holiday Association, was "undermining the revolution," and therefore was "an enemy of the working class."[18]

At the same time, the news trickling down from Russia was disturbing. Stalin's rise to power in the late 1920s was one of unparalleled repression. Rodney, and other radicals like him, who assumed after Lenin's death that Trotsky would be in power in Russia, felt betrayed. Not only was Trotsky not a successor to Lenin, he had been forced out of power and fled Russia, fearing for his life. Stalin's purges continued. The dream of agrarian reform was brutalized by the knowledge of what was happening in Mother Russia. The intellectuals, writers, or anyone who protested the power of the state, were suspect, and were either executed, banished to Siberia, or fled the country. The disparity between the ideals of Communism and a free, unified world, and the reality of trying to attain them, proved insurmountable. The idea that, to achieve this new vision there would be the necessary deaths for the revolution, was beyond what radicals like my father could tolerate. The ends, finally, could not justify the bloody means.

There were troubled waters at the local level in Plentywood, too, with a split between the Stalinists and the Trotskyites, which often erupted in fights and bitter quarreling. As a result, these philosophical differences created more confusion in the community at large, and weakened the Communist argument as they competed against one another for the minds and votes of the electorate. One sad example was between old friends Hans Rasmussen and Rodney. Apparently in a fit of righteous anger, Rodney, a Trotskyite, confronted Hans, a Stalinist, and they came to blows. It happened at the office of *The Producers News*, where Hans was the business manager. The editor at the time stopped the confrontation.[19] Rodney Salisbury and Hans Rasmussen, comrades for years, lost their friendship because of this break in the local party.

This reminds me of a time many years later when some old friends from Plentywood came to visit. They were sitting at the kitchen table in Arlee, reminiscing about old times. I was a young girl reading, but mostly listening to them, fascinated because these people were from the magical world of the ranch, the prairie, the mythical town of the forever name, "Plentywood." They mention names that I am familiar with, a regular litany of my mother's past. Homer, a writer and newspaper man, said, "By the early thirties, Marie, we were all disillusioned Communists, and considered ourselves Trotskyites. Hans Rasmussen surprised us all, didn't he? He talked the party line, was a devout Stalinist, and believed the ends justified the means. Even Max Eastman, whom we all revered and trusted, not only as a poet and good writer, but because he was great Socialist and took a stand against war, couldn't budge Hans. How could we help but be surprised? Hans knew, as we all did, that Max returned from Russia feeling that the revolution had been subverted by corrupt leaders. Remember how we all, including Hans, read his book, his translation of Leon Trotsky's *History of the Russian Revolution*?

There was a pause. *Rodney tried,* my mother said. *His fight with Hans, when they came to blows, couldn't pound it out of him, either. Only proved Rod could lose a friendship.* There was quiet laughter. *Rodney never quit missing him, you know. Couldn't quit talking about him, either.* The room was quiet.

As for the Communist Party, it vacillated between kicking detractors out of the party, and then later, some other official would reinstate them. There were threats, but somehow people like Rodney Salisbury and Charlie Taylor were still hanging on, though suspected always of deviating from the party line and going rogue. Taylor, a Trotskyite, was asked by the party to rein in the Trotskyites of Plentywood, and Taylor dutifully (and amazingly) sent a letter to *The Producers News* asking that they come back into the fold and vote for the Communists in the election campaign.[20] By this time, there was little of the radical spirit left in Plentywood, and Taylor's voice was muted by his absence, the loss of focus and local vision, and the shifting national scene with FDR. Taylor eventually returned to Plentywood and *The Producers News*, but the climate had changed, and the voice of the *News* was not sustainable in this new era. Most of the advertising was going to the *Plentywood Herald*, and though Taylor pleaded for his subscribers to pay up so he could pay his help, it didn't happen. In March 1937, after almost twenty years, the paper pulled down the blinds, stopped the press, and locked the door. It was the end of an era. The paper and the colorful "Red Flag" Taylor now belonged to history.

Harry Polk, the contentious editor of the *Plentywood Herald* and rival of *The Producers News*, in a superb twist of irony, wrote the obituary. He was generous, and gave credit to a paper that livened the discourse among the Plentywood citizens. "The discontinuation of *The Producers News* closed an eventful career of many years. It rose to great heights, and then fell. . . . Of all the newspapers started in Sheridan County, and now suspended, *The Producers News* had the most colorful career."[21]

30

I once asked my half-sister Camilla about our father, what he was like as a dad, as a man. She adored Rodney and talked about how playful he was, how he laughed at a good joke, even on himself, how he liked to invite friends over for whiskey and cigars. "The talk," she said, "both serious and full of light and laughter would go on until the early hours of the morning. The smell of coffee was the signal they would soon eat a big breakfast, and leave to go home in time for chores." She always made a point of talking about how honest he was, and I would just listen. But what I found most interesting in what she had to say was how he had times of quiet, meditative solitude. "During these times," she said, "you knew better than to interrupt him, or try to get his attention. He was thinking, worried, sorting things out."

I can imagine those times, what they meant, maybe because my brother Budson has that melancholy bent, too, when he is troubled.

There is something tragic about this time in the life of my father. His boundless energy and fight for justice had left him adrift in a new era, where he was not the wunderkind organizer, friend of the common man, favorite in the community he loved. And that's not the end of it. When Rodney and Marie's baby girl was nine months old, Marie was pregnant, again.

It was all coming apart, and the radical farm movement had a frayed and fragile existence in Plentywood. Rodney, Marie, Andrew, Emma, and all their children suffered because of this affair, in addition to the economic hardships of farm life in the plains, of the Depression years when everything looked bleak. Circumstances dictated change, and life as they had known and experienced it was vanishing into the future. I can imagine the mixed feelings of Rodney and Marie as they contemplated leaving the prairie country of Plentywood with its stark beauty, it's implacable, changeable weather, a country where hard work yielded success at the throw of the dice. The old camaraderie was gone, as well as their dream for a more just future brought about by their passion and dedication. That intense, hopeful time was carved into indelible memory. At the same time, they were relieved and glad to be leaving and starting a life somewhere else, some place where they were not known, and able to enjoy freedom without scrutiny. To just be.

I think of Andrew Hansen, how this man, married a few years and with two young children, was mentally and emotionally abandoned by the woman he married and perhaps loved. He had so much that was good in him. That I discovered. My mother and father disrupted many lives, including their own, for what they believed to be an "authentic existence," outside the norms of conventional life.

My mother, finally, was able to get a divorce from Andrew Hansen before this last baby was born. It was a rancorous divorce, and several times she told me that, pregnant with Roger, desperate, she went to the mill and pleaded, begged, and screamed at him to divorce her. I'm quite sure she regaled him with the fact that Budson, Jo Anne, and the child she was carrying were not his children, but her lover's, Rodney. She was outcast and desperate. During one of their quarrels, he shoved her out the door, and she fell down the stairs. I had the sense that she felt vulnerable, and he took advantage of her. I can also guess that in her desperation she was uncontrollable, frenzied. This episode my mother repeated to me many times, and I could always see that it had embittered her forever against Andrew. But now, considering it all, I think it was the stipulations he demanded of her in order to grant her a divorce that made her bitter and caused their unspeakable quarrels. He would give her a sum of money, he said, but he would keep his children, Jim and Anneva. They would not be a part of the divorce settlement, and they would not go with her and Rodney to their new home in Billings. He also wanted Budson to stay with the only family he knew, and the man he thought of as his father, Andrew. To add to my mother's misery, he and Leora Wine tried to steal the baby girl away. They had grown fond of this child and wanted to keep her.

We were leaving for Billings, and we went to the Wolf Point house to get you. Andrew and Leora were driving away with you. I stood there, scream-ing, pounding on the window. I picked up a rock, and threw it at the car.

"Give me my baby," I kept screaming. Rodney waved Andrew down, and they stopped. Rodney took you from Leora's arms. God, they were miserable bastards, just miserable. They would have taken you away, kept you. As if we didn't have any rights to our child.

She hesitated, smiled a little, lit another cigarette.

Of course, they had convinced themselves that I was an unfit mother. Leora Wine couldn't have children, and she wanted you. Oh, yes, by this time, she was living at the house with Andrew, my hired girl and that ignorant old shrew of a mother of hers, Mrs. McCauley. God, they were such lowbrows. I will say one thing, though. Leora wanted to marry Andrew, so she helped talk him into a divorce. They married sometime later, and this ignorant woman was the mother of my children, Jim and Anneva. She was all the wickedness you can think of as a stepmother. Jimmy started running away from home, missing school. Anneva was sometimes mocked as being like her mother.

Then she would cry, the deep sorrow of her invaded the house, and we, her present children, were forgotten.

Andrew gave Marie a sum of money. How much, I never heard, though it has been hinted that it was a substantial amount. In the late fall of 1934, Marie and Rodney left Plentywood for Billings, Montana. It is rumored that before she left, she went to the house in Wolf Point and took all of the furniture with her, except for what was in Jim and Anneva's rooms.

Whatever amount Andrew gave her, it was enough money to buy a house in Billings. I still remember the address: 901 North 22nd Street. It was a small house with an unfinished upstairs and a big friendly cottonwood tree in the front yard. The North Side Park was two blocks away, and the North Side School was just a block beyond that. There, in Billings at that address, is where I eventually grew into a consciousness of my world and the people around me. I was eighteen months old when my little brother, Roger, was born in the Billings Deaconess Hospital on March 24, 1935. My mother had a story about this, one I heard many times.

It was a tiresome pregnancy, going on and on and on, through the fall, the winter . . . the longest of all. The divorce, the move from Plentywood, all those ties were gone. And all that misery, too . . . funny, but you can miss misery, too. It reminds you that you're alive, I suppose. I missed the prairie, Pet, you can't imagine . . . the beauty of it, the feral wildness. Here we were, a family of sorts, in this new town. We had some friends in Billings, old union organizers, radicals like us, classless, and that was a godsend. Budson was a problem, always wanting to go back to Andrew, resenting his father, Rodney, getting into trouble. It was not a good time for another baby, and here I was, big and clumsy, trying to fit our life in this new place. We hadn't been in Billings but a few months when my water broke, and Rodney took me to the hospital, Billings Deaconess. You were eighteen months old, just walking and getting into everything.

Somewhere in her stories she always paused, lit another cigarette, opened a beer or poured more coffee, leaned on the counter and looked out the window. And saw what? Her inner landscape of painful memory, of clouded visions of happiness, of her youth, trouble-free, searching the wild expanse of prairie for nature's treasures? The story she was telling brought her back, the art of it, giving me the past in the present—and here I am, taking stock, writing a memoir, keeping the faith of her, my sad, bitter, disillusioned mother, finding solace in the retelling, the artistry of her story, her way of making sense of a confused, tumultuous life of love.

I was having trouble having this baby. Through the fog of pain, Rodney came to tell me they wanted to do a caesarean section, right then. Next thing I knew I was wheeling down a hall, and woke up in pain, with a baby. I was too weak to see him, and then I got an infection in the incision. I was in the hospital for three months . . . three months!

I died. I know it's hard to believe, but I tell you, I died. I know it. I was on the third floor of the hospital, and I could see the tops of the old pine trees out the window. I floated out the window, and I was there in the breeze gently moving among those trees . . . yes, I was still in bed. It was peaceful, so easy . . . just floating, just surrendering, just being . . .

At this point in the narrative, my mother was always awestruck, amazed, that she had died, and yet here she was, telling the tale.

I came back to excited voices all around me, the doctors and nurses, tense, doing things, bringing me back. I slowly got well after that. When Rodney brought Roger in to see me, he was sitting up with a spit curl on his forehead.

I didn't know him, this strange child of my misfortune. Rodney came and took us home.

Here, my mother smiled, remembering. *I put on my red tam, gave it that little jerk to make it slant the right way, and Rodney smiled, looked relieved, had tears in his eyes. "You're back, Marie. The hat, the way you put it on. That's you, your old self."*

31

Other changes were happening as well. Soon after Marie and Rodney moved to Billings, Emma Salisbury changed her mind and decided she had struggled enough with farming, and wanted to leave Plentywood with her family. Life was hard for her there on several levels: farming the ranch was difficult with the lack of rain, the hard times, even with the help of the older children and New Deal jobs. The sympathy she aroused as an abandoned wife was not only embarrassing, but also degrading.

Every day was a struggle, and the future looked tenuous in Plentywood. Many were leaving this hard land. The radicals in Plentywood were losing ground, and their children were often taunted as "Reds" and "godless heathens." Emma also lived with the constant betrayal of her husband and her former friend, Marie. It was an uneasy role for her, which Rodney understood. He felt sympathy for her plight, and accountable, too. He had brought his young bride to Raymond to homestead, and they had been excited and hopeful, envisioning a promising life, raising a family, doing the necessary hard work to make their dreams come true on the high plains of Montana. She not only supported all of his radical ideas, but she agreed with them, and in this respect they were like-minded. They had their children, another common interest. Mike, the oldest son, was playing jazz piano all over the state, riding the wave of the Jazz Age. Gene, their second-oldest son, was thinking of law school, Jardis and Camilla were in high school and would soon need college, as would Patty, their youngest child. It was time for change and no looking back. Friends were moving on, trying their luck somewhere else. There was only the time ahead, the future and what it would unveil. The family had concluded that the most logical place to move was to Missoula, where jobs were more plentiful, and where the university was.

I asked my sister Camilla how Emma and the Salisbury family were able to move to Missoula in the middle of the Depression and buy a home. She mentioned, rather casually, that Rodney had insured the house in

Plentywood and set it on fire. "It burned to the ground like a tinder box. It was gone in a matter of minutes," she stated matter-of-factly. "He gave the insurance money and the money from selling the ranch to Mother. When we left, Mother had the body of Janis exhumed, and she came with us. She's buried in the cemetery in Missoula. We bought a small house in Orchard Homes, and we survived by raising a garden, picking fruit, and mother worked for the WPA."

The Missoula phone book had a listing of "Mrs. Rodney Salisbury." In Emma's several moves, this was always the listing until she died. She was implacable to the end: the wife with the name, the "Mrs.," even though after 1934, Rodney never lived with her again.

The families were all dispersed, their radical revolutionary days behind them. They had moved to milder, less dramatic, climates in every sense of the word. Billings and Missoula were lovely places to raise gardens, and both Marie and Emma were ardent gardeners. It helped them survive those tough Depression years before World War II. I remember my mother putting together bunches of carrots, radishes, beets, bags of string beans and peas, and putting them in my doll buggy. Roger and I would go door to door selling this fresh produce for five cents a bunch, but without much luck.

I find myself often wondering how my parents survived during those first years in Billings. They were grassroots organizers, and my mother was a newspaper woman. They chose to live in a society peopled with intellectuals, artists, writers of the time, liberals, and organizers. But they had no jobs. They both came from the rural life of ranching and farming. They were the "proletariat." Their time was also an era when learning and a formal education were desired and important goals. My mother had been married to a prosperous man whose family owned acres of wheat land and flour mills dotted along the small towns of the Hi-Line in eastern Montana. As a married woman, she had enjoyed financial security. Rodney had been a farmer-rancher, sheriff, restaurant owner, bootlegger. These sources of revenue had sputtered out. Here they were, exiles, in Billings, Montana, adrift from close ties of family and friends, with three children to support. I can only think it must have been a daunting time for them, so much change and loss, and their passionate path had moved them here to this town to begin anew. I cannot imagine that they were without hope. I cannot.

It seemed like all the rush of the world disappeared when we moved to Billings. We bought the house, paid cash. It was like after all those years in Plentywood, I learned how to breathe again. Rodney found this squeaky old rocking chair in an alley, cleaned it up and painted it a dark cherry, and gave it to me. "Your throne," he said. Lazy and pregnant, I'd sit in it and rock squeak, rock squeak, reading magazines to you. You'd sit on my lap, and I would take Cosmopolitan, *or* Life, *and turn the pages, telling you stories about the people on each page. I'd say, "This man just bought a new hat, and he's happy and so . . . " and I'd turn another page, and there might be a wom-en cooking at a stove, "and so he met this woman, whose name was Mabel," and I'd turn a page . . . "and so they bought a car . . . and so . . . "*

If I hesitated too long, you'd urge "and so, and so . . ."

When I came home from the hospital after recovering from Roger's birth, you were almost two. Rodney took you everywhere with him, and I was the stranger. I would try to take you on my lap, but you struggled and cried, and wanted Rodney. One day, I got a magazine, held you, though you were struggling, and began to read to you. "And so," I said. You stopped struggling. "And so," you looked at me, "and so," then said, "Mama!"

We were home.

Rodney has thrown a rope over a branch of the big old cottonwood tree in the front yard, and made a swing. The car is parked in its summer shade. The three of us take turns while Rodney pushes us. The limb is high, and the swing has a wide arc. The whole Rimrock neighborhood is a tantaliz-ing, momentary glimpse. We squabble over whose turn it is.

They are getting ready to leave again. They are on the road, organizing. In the early morning light, my mother bends down to me. Her auburn hair aglow, her deep-blue eyes look into mine. She smells of perfume and cigarettes. She opens her large purse, and finds a stick of spearmint gum. Her fingers, tipped with rose-colored polish, tear the gum in half. She carefully unwraps one small piece, and puts it in my mouth. My mother!

We have a goat named Socrates, a most miserable creature, who eats clothes off the line, and tin cans when he can find them. In the early morning hours I get up and go outside. Socrates meets me at the door, chases me around the yard, butting me all the way. Crying and screaming, I slap him on the nose. His stubborn amber eyes with crosses in them are hard as Lucifer's. Budson rescues me, laughing. "You've got to think like a goat," he says. I admire his big-brother wisdom.

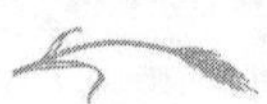

32

I found something, though, that gave me an insight on just how bad the times were, and how Rodney and Marie were trying to survive, mostly by their wits. I feel shame for them, and maybe they felt that way, too, but I can only guess. Maybe, for them, it was just an adventure that they were in together, driven by necessity, maybe even desperation, but with an element of exhilarating fun and daring.

I don't remember how I originally ran across this article, which is in my archives. It is from the *Plentywood Herald*, August 29, 1935, and was taken from the *Conrad News*. I can imagine the relish that the *Herald*'s editor, Harry Polk, had upon finding this article in the Conrad paper, since it affirmed all his animosity toward Salisbury, Taylor, and the rival paper, *The Producers News*. At the time, Budson was seven, I was two, and my brother Roger was a baby five months old.

"Last Thursday, Conrad was visited by a couple of solicitors, who introduced themselves as Mrs. R. Marie Hansen, authorized agent of the Holiday Association and Mr. Salisbury, state president of the same association." The article goes on to say that they called on several local businessmen soliciting advertising in the Farm Holiday pamphlet, which was to be distributed to seventeen hundred farmers. Marie, a newspaper woman, knew the ropes of selling advertising. She had a dummy paper with her, with pages marked out for ads—a whole page, half-page, quarter-page— which she would show the prospective customer. She would suggest how the ad might be written to entice people to buy from that business. The cost of each ad, and what it could do, was discussed at great length. She acted like the professional she was. The article suggested that if the business didn't buy an ad, there were veiled threats of a boycott, presumably from farmers in their locale. Also, all ads sold were to be paid for in advance, though some wanted to wait until a pamphlet was in their hands. Farmers Union members got note of this activity and began checking it out. A Mrs. Kay, state junior leader of the union, happened to be in Lewistown at the same time the couple were working that city, and said they were practically run out of town. Later, in Conrad, the same thing happened.

Previous to this article in the *Conrad News*, a Farmers Union meeting in Billings in July had heard there were people soliciting advertising in their name, and the secretary was to send a warning to all counties. They were advised that this couple had no authority to use the Farmers Union in their soliciting. Even more telling, the Conrad area was not attached to the Farm Holiday Association, which was stronger in eastern Montana and the Dakotas during its brief life span of a few years. Worse, the receipt book that the couple used was for North Dakota and dated 1934. A line was drawn through the date and place, and Montana and the current date were substituted. Was this arrogance, or were they just too broke to get an authentic receipt book? Did they intend to publish these ads, but needed the money to live? The Conrad union members worked fast, and by the time Rodney and Marie went to the bank to cash the checks, the payments were stopped. All the sheriffs in the state were notified, as were the county attorneys. "All the sheriffs"—the irony here is apparent.

In an old trunk in the attic I found several peach-colored pamphlets, titled "The Farm Holiday Association." It was the Christmas edition. Those pamphlets, vestiges of a veiled past, are gone now, but the way I felt when I found them remains. I looked at them often, a girl discovering her father. It made me proud that my father was listed as president, and my mother as secretary. It made them seem like important, responsible people, who had a special place in the world. It was full of ads, as I remember, and articles about the union and union members. There was also this poem, submitted by Marie for this Christmas edition, which I also found in my archives. It expresses her bent toward romantic sentimentality. It is, I recognize, a villanelle, a form of poetry, and I have copied it here in that form.

Season's Greetings
The West is Dead

What path is left for you to tread

When hungry wolves are slinking near—
Do you know the west is dead?

The working man now packs his bed
Along the trails of yesteryear—
What path is left for you to tread?
Your fathers, golden sunset led
To virgin prairies wide and clear
Do you not know the west is dead?

New dismal cities rise instead
And freedom is not there nor here
What path is left for you to tread?

Your father's world for which they bled
Is fenced and settled far and near—
Do you not know the west is dead?

Your father gained a crust of bread,
Their bones bleach on the lost frontier;
What path is left for you to tread?
Do you not know the west is dead?

RALPH CHAPLIN

There were also several pages of "Holiday Association of Montana" stationery, with the names of the executive committee, all familiar in the many contexts of my mother's fond memories of Plentywood friends, such as J. F. Kramlick, Jerome C. Locke, Leverne Hamilton, Art Wankle. Several lovely dresses, still smelling faintly of perfume, as well as a pin-striped navy-blue suit, were carefully folded in a corner. Three silk blouses, a frilly pale yellow, a cream-colored satin, and a bright blue, were wrapped in tissue. These remnants of her previous life never left their hiding place there in that old trunk in the attic. They belonged to a mother I didn't know.

Also in this trunk were small books called "Blue Books." Shakespeare's *Hamlet*, as well as philosophy by Will Durant and writings by Robert Ingersol, were in residence, all with the elegant signature, Rodney Salisbury. Camilla remarked that these little books were cheap, easily fit in one's pocket, and had a variety of subjects, ranging from great works of literature to books about religion and sex. She said they were popular, and their family bought and read them regularly. I am reminded that Emma Goldman always carried a book with her in case she was arrested.

33

Rodney was still trying to get a divorce, but Emma's resistance did not falter. They kept hoping, meanwhile carrying on their day-to-day lives. According to my mother, because of his experiences with organizing and the Farmer Labor Movement in all of its manifestations, he was asked to lecture at Rocky Mountain College in Billings, and perhaps he was paid a stipend for doing so. Too, they were on the road a lot, and left us with housekeepers. As I came into greater consciousness, there was Ada and Joe, a black couple, who were familiar figures from that time. Joe was to take care of the garden, flowers, and lawn, and Ada was in charge of the house, our clothes, and cooking. When our parents were gone, sometimes they would have parties and invite their friends. The kitchen would be crowded and noisy with wild dancing, singing, and laughing until late at night. On such nights, we stayed up, and people would take turns dancing with Roger and me. I remember the uneasy terror of Ada tilting the lid on the kitchen stove until it rocked, saying, "Dat's de debil in de fire." There was a neighbor, old and stooped, who slowly passed our house each day. Of him she would say, "He's de man who grabs young chillens and takes 'em away when de bad." Roger and I would be scared, but Budson, when we told him, just scoffed, and said Ada was "a crazy old witch and nutty in her head from practicing voodoo."

Rodney and Marie were concerned always about making a living. They were trying to figure out some way of making the economy work for them, and visiting places where this might happen. There was something nomadic about them, unsettled, wandering, always going someplace. We were waving them goodbye, or we were excited they were home, bringing us presents. I have snippets of memory, sharp and clear of that time: a flood that brought them hurrying home to find the basement full of water and canned jars of fruit and vegetables floating merrily about; a visit to the lumberyard and the piney smell that still, to this day, evokes visions of my father. I am astride his shoulders, hanging on to his nappy hair, and he is singing a happy tune. He builds me a playhouse, complete with orange crates for cupboards, for my fifth birthday; laughter and excitement of a party wake me up, and together, they bring me hot chocolate with marshmallows; the earaches that make me wake up crying, and they take me into their bed, and Mom blows smoke in my aching ears until I fall asleep.

During this time Pete Steinov, their old IWW friend from Plentywood, came for a visit. It was Easter, when I was about five, that I first remember him. Rodney, Marie, and Pete stayed up late, talking, drinking beer, and laughing. He took Roger and me to the park and pushed us so high in the swings that I got scared and cried. Later he visited Emma and her family in Missoula, and passed on the latest news of us. He told them that Rodney's little girl, Jo Anne, poor little tyke, was sickly, not quite right in her head.

Our Billings house is the first place that I have of stored memories. We had no phone, but the neighbors next door to us did, and sometimes one of them would come and tell my father or mother they had a call. Our house had electricity and running water, but an outdoor toilet. There was a boardwalk leading to a small house in the back where Ada and Joe stayed. Rodney taught me how to dance, "salap, salap," on that walk, and we did simple routines together. These early lessons were the beginning of many dance lessons through my youth, and, like my father, I loved to dance and have enjoyed it all of my life. At some point, there was a gas stove. I got up one summer morning and decided to bake something, as I had seen my mother do. I turned on the gas, lit a match, and held it to the spot where it would light the oven. It surprised me by flashing out, and caught fire to my hair, eyebrows and eyelashes. I ran for my parents' bed, jumped under the covers, screaming all the way. I don't remember their reaction, though I can imagine, but I do remember that my brother Budson, every time he saw me, jeered at how funny I looked. "You look naked and very awful, like something out of a Frankenstein movie," he said. I cried.

Ada and Joe were with us for a long time, as I dimly recall, and sometime during this period there was talk that Rodney and Marie went to Mexico to see Trotsky. In my historical searching, I found a picture of Trotsky, when he arrived in Mexico with his wife and was met by Frieda

Kahlo and Max Shachtman, the U.S. leader of the Trotskyites, who lived in New York, a friend of Rodney and Marie's. The year was January 1937. My mother mentioned it, at various times, but it was not a memorable story for me. Budson says they went to Mexico, but they didn't see Trotsky. What I do know is that we had a signed picture of Trotsky taken when he was in Mexico and living with the artists Frieda Kahlo and Diego Rivera. It rests, as I write this, in a frame on my bookcase. The writing is faded and old, barely discernable.

The tensions of Trotsky's last years escaping death threats from Moscow left him with high blood pressure and thoughts of suicide. Looking over the choices he had made in his life, he said he had no regrets and would do it all over again. I am reminded of my father, Rodney, when Trotsky concluded before his death, "I shall die a proletarian revolutionist, a Marxist, a dialectical materialist and, consequently, an irreconcilable atheist."[22]

34

It is spring in Billings, lush with verdant green and splashes of color. It is June 1938. Pansies, roses, peonies, irises are in full regalia. In my memory, the neighbor woman is at the door, telling my mother she has a phone call. An image, desperate, swift, of my mother running across the garden to the little gate and disappearing into the house next door, is a permanent presence in my mind to this day, as is her story of heartbreak, told over and over again in her lovely, timbred voice.

He was going to Plentywood and see if he could collect some owed debts. Mike was having some troubles with his young wife, Karenina. She was one of my hired girls, you know, a sweet person. He got her pregnant, so that determined his future, especially in those days. Emma was going to Plentywood, too, because Mike, it was rumored, was leaving Karenina and their two little girls for a new girlfriend, a girl named Tula Lund. Rodney was disgusted with Mike, as he often was, and Emma was concerned, and wanted her oldest and favorite son to do the right thing. The divorce was on his mind, too. Rodney was sure that this time, Emma would give him a divorce. She would finally release him, he thought, because their children were grown and going out on their own. You would be six in August. It was important to your father that you and your two brothers have his name. That was his hope, every time.

She paused. Her silence went on, and I just waited. I was used to this story, and how it unfolded, and somehow, never tired of it. Having our father's name meant a lot to all of us, even Budson. A memory of that time is of playing with the little girl next door, she on her side of the fence, I on mine. We would dig under the fence, and make piles of dirt and weave stories around them. One day she came and told me, "My mother says I can't play with you anymore, because you are a bastard." I must have asked my mother and father what this meant. I don't remember being very concerned, but I'm sure they were. I kept going to the fence, anyway, thinking she might return.

That day, the day he was leaving, I fixed fried eggs, just the way he liked them, over-easy. "Come with me, Mairizie . . . please me in this, I don't want to be missing you right now." But I just laughed at him, and told him I wanted to do "wifely" things like make strawberry jam and paint the kitchen. A comment like this would usually make him laugh, but not this time. "Oh, Rodney, you'll be back in just a few days, and Emma doesn't really have any reason not to give us a divorce now. She's in another town. Her kids are not little any more."

He picked up his suitcase, that old worn leather bag of his that had seen so many journeys. I helped him on with his coat, hugged him. I was anxious to get out into the garden, pick those spring berries.

It was this next part, the part I knew so well, had grown so familiar with it seemed as if I were there when it happened.

He walked out the door toward the car, his belt trailing behind him. Then he turned back to me, those long strides of his, pulled me into his arms and held me . . . held me, not saying anything, and then, his belt still dragging, got in the car and drove off. That is the last memory I have of him.

When my mother finished this story, she always left the room, maybe to go to bed to read and forget, maybe to the post office, or the garden, or the bar. The three of us were never sure when she would return.

Sometimes, after this story, I would sit there, thinking about other possible and happier endings. That he had survived and come back to us.

The story I know of that time is that when my mother received the phone call from the neighbors, it was an old friend from Plentywood, Hans Rasmussen, who had called to tell her Rodney was in the hospital in Plentywood. Ralph Rich, a union organizer and friend from Billings, took her to Plentywood to be with Rodney before he died. They drove all day, and it got dark. *"What time is it?"* my mother asked him. "11:30," Ralph answered. My mother says her hair stood on end. She knew he was dead. Ralph Rich, she reported, looked at her in shocked surprise: "Good god, Marie! Are you alright?"

She was right. By the time they got to Plentywood and went to the hospital, Rodney was gone. He had been there three days, paralyzed, unable to speak. He wrote unreadable notes, trying desperately to communicate his last thoughts. Finally, on the third day, late in the afternoon, he lapsed into a coma and died that night. His wife, Emma, and the Salisbury children had been with him at the end. She had his body removed to the Labor Temple for his memorial service. When my mother went to the Labor Temple where he was to be honored, she was stopped at the door. Emma, a few of her friends, and the Salisbury children turned her away, refusing to let her come in and attend his funeral. His other family claimed him in the end, and she was left out, this woman who had been his partner for almost thirteen years, and with whom he had had three children. She rarely spoke of this time, and when she did, her anguish made her speech slow and halting. No story she could tell would encompass the misery and loss she felt.

Rumors surrounded my father in death as they had in life. It was said that he got in a barroom brawl in Plentywood and hit his head, and that's how he happened to have a brain hemorrhage. The doctors attending him said no, there was no blow to indicate violence. The worst rumor, which circulated some time later, was that Marie had poisoned him. How virulent was the hatred directed at my mother for her attachment to this man! How it must have withered the spirit of this wild, precocious, romantic prairie girl!

When Rodney died, the *Plentywood Herald*, the only paper now in Plentywood, had the following to say: "Probably no other man in Sheridan County has been on the lips of friend and foe as Rodney Salisbury. His enemies and others bitterly condemn his past activities. Friends today said he was fearless in his convictions and that he was no lover of sham. His fight, they say, was for the underdog."

But it was Max Shachtman, leader of the Trotskyites, who wrote the most laudatory testimony of all. Pete Gallagher and John Boulds, old friends and comrades of Rodney's, let Max Shachtman know of Rodney's death. In the *Socialist Appeal* of June 1938, in an article titled "A Veteran Passes," he wrote the following: "The death of this model revolutionary came as an especially rude blow to those of us in New York—Jim Cannon, Marty Abern and myself—who had known and esteemed him since the early days of the communist movement." The article further elaborated by saying, "From the early founding of Sheridan County, which was later to become Montana's 'red county,' he was a familiar figure in and around Plentywood. For years, he was among the leading spirits fighting weekly for Montana's workers and farmers, *The Producers News*, and a prominent leader in every progressive movement." Shachtman went on to extol Rodney by saying, "There never was a more unique sheriff in the United States, for his jail was plastered with the posters of the International Red Aid, the International Defense Aid, and the Mooney Defense Committee. Many a homeless and hungry migratory worker learned that Rodney's 'Jail' was far more like a hotel for the night." Shachtman closed the tribute to Rodney by remembering the family, but before he did, he said one final defining thing about him: "Hard-headed and tough-fisted militant that he was, he had no lack of ability to fight for his views. That is why he could not reconcile himself with Stalinism, and joined our movement in the early days. The bureaucrats hated and feared him, and they had good cause."

So Rodney Salisbury died, a man of his time, and lived on in memory. He is buried in the Missoula County Cemetery. In 2010, as part of the Stories and Stones Reenactment Project, actor Don Spritzer resurrected the Communist sheriff of Plentywood, assumed his persona, and garnered much applause for his excellent performance.

One of Rodney's favorite sayings, which my mother often quoted, illustrates his political awareness of the time: *Russian totalitarianism will bore from within and destroy Democratic institutions. It will take over without firing a shot.*

35

My father Rodney died in June 1938. That August 19th, I had my fifth birthday. My brother Roger was three in March of that same year. Budson was ten. Despite all of Marie and Rodney's efforts, none of us carried the name of our true father; Andrew Hansen's name was carried by all of Marie Chapman Hansen's children.

When my mother left Plentywood for that last time, barred from honoring the man who was the love of her life, she faced a bleak, uncertain future. Aside from working as a typesetter for the *Plentywood Herald* as a young girl and as a part-time stringer for the Associated Press for several years, she had never had a job. Rodney's legal wife, Emma, claimed the car and all of his worldly goods. Nig Collins, the owner of the Chicken Farm bar and brothel, had been forced to give up his business, and he willed the land and buildings to Rodney. These, in turn, went to Emma. My mother was left with three children to raise, no money, no job, and no support of any kind.

There is a story of that time that she told me. I don't remember when I first heard it, but I know I heard it more than once—much more. It is a story of a five-year-old girl who does not understand death, but she understands loss.

It was impossible, those first days, weeks, months. . . . You drove me crazy, Jode, waiting for your father. You would sit on the front step, and when you saw a gray car drive by, you would run and find me and, excited, tell me "Nonny's coming. His car is out there . . . I saw it!" Of course, when you pulled me to the door to see, the car was gone, and you'd say, "Maybe he had to go around the block. Maybe he had to buy something."

You didn't lose hope for a long time. I would try to explain that he wasn't coming back, that he had to go away for a long time to do something, but you took up your vigil all that summer. There weren't all the different colors and models of cars then, just gray, black, and tan sedans, I think. So many cars passed each day that looked exactly like Rodney's car, and you were just sure he would stop one day, and get out of the car, and swing you up in the air, saying "How's my girl? I missed you!"

One day, another car, gray, like Rodney's, with a man driving slowed up before our house. You were so excited, and you ran screaming to find me, "Nonny's here! I told you he would come home. He's here!" When we got to the front step, the car was pulling away, and soon was out of sight. You stood for a long time, watching that car disappear. Then you said, "I guess he doesn't want to come here anymore."

And that was the last time you stood your vigil, waiting for a father that never returned.

In my mind, those first three years after Rodney died, and before we moved to the reservation at Arlee, are fragments of troubled, chaotic times. I cannot connect the sequence of events, but there are unforgettable images. One is of Andrew showing up in his gray coupe. This man with whom she had such a rancorous divorce came to help her. He came because he knew she was broke, and in trouble. Budson was happy to see him, and I remember Andrew calling Budson "son." Andrew, Marie, and Budson all went shopping and returned with groceries, and new clothes for the three of us, as well as school supplies. Pencils, tablets, and large boxes of crayons were new and exciting, and Budson, a future artist, never forgot the drawing pencils and paints that Andrew gave him. I loved the pink-checked dress with round white buttons down the front and the little pink purse. We were happy to see him, for in the confused world in which we lived, he was like another father. For Budson, he was the only real one. Before he left, Andrew took a picture of the three of us, and another one of me under the plum tree. It was one of the few pictures of us together as children. When he left, we gathered around the car, and hugged him and waved goodbye. That day, at least, our mother was easy with him, perhaps because she had appreciated that he was dependable and she was grateful. She had needed him, and he was there for her.

I realize now that he also had her children, Jim and Anneva, and he had not brought them with him. One of my sharpest and most persistent memories from my growing consciousness is of my mother weeping, talking about the brother and sister who did not live with us. Andrew must have promised, though, that they would come and visit. That was the only time I know of that he came to see us, though it was not the last time we saw him. Jim and Anneva came separately that next summer and fall.

Years later, I told my brother Jim about this visit. I was surprised when he said, "In spite of everything, the old man cared for her."

My brother Roger, about three years old, is with me. We have walked hand in hand to the North Side Park to play on the swings and merry go 'round. I look at him, and see him for the first time. He has on a yellow sunsuit and a white shirt with a yellow duck on the front. His hair is shiny copper, and his large blue eyes are fringed with golden-tipped, curly lashes. There is a sprinkle of freckles across his nose. I know, in my young mind, that he is beautiful, and that we both are very new to this old world. The smell of chlorine from the swimming pool, the hot sun on the fresh lilacs, the smell of sweet clover, and my senses know that we are among the living.

He's gone, and there is no pattern to anything. There is nothing that can be counted on, nothing for sure. Mealtimes are haphazard. There is no food in the house, and Roger and I are sent to the store a few blocks down the street to get day-old bread for a nickel. The dirty clothes pile up. We can't find underwear, matching socks, clean shirts or dresses. The taxi driver, Alex, young and handsome, comes late at night with beer or wine, and they sit at the kitchen table for hours, talking. She cries, wails the loss of her lover, of her two children, Jim and Anneva. Budson is angry, difficult, unruly. He has skipped the third grade, and the fifth grade. He is precocious, verbal, clever. His outbursts of temper are directed at Alex, and finally, Alex leaves for good. Worried about Budson because he is hanging out with a wild crowd of boys who wander the streets of Billings looking for trouble, Marie takes him to a psychiatrist. She cannot manage or control him, even less since Rodney's death. After several visits, the psychiatrist tells her that Budson has the brilliant mind of a criminal, and he needs to get away from Billings and bad influences. Budson is privy to this information, and outlives it, but it is a hurtful and negative prophecy.

Our mother is sleeping during the day, roaming the house at night, drinking, crying, talking to herself. A fragment: She is an unforgettable image there at the top of the stairs, dressed in a cobalt-blue satin gown tied at her narrow waist with a belt with tassels of bright pink roses. Her dark blue eyes are startling, her auburn hair aglow. Below, we are standing in chronological order: Budson, Jo Anne, Roger, looking up at her.

I can't live without your father. It's no use. I can't do it. I have to leave you. Budson, take care of your brother and sister, and don't let anyone separate you.

"Please don't go. We'll be good, Mama," Roger says.

I am quiet inside, everything is still, and I am waiting. Budson rounds the newel post, runs up the stairs, and gets her. "You're tired, Mom. Come to bed now."

There were times in our youth when the three of us talked about what we remembered about our father. It was sketchy, at best. Budson, the oldest, did not have tender memories of Rodney. Budson loved to fish, and he recalled how Rodney and Marie would drop him off at the Yellowstone River and wouldn't return to get him until it was dark. Eight years old, alone and afraid, he would huddle on the bank, waiting to see the light of their car to take him to safety. The lap of the waves, the rustle in the trees, the muted sounds of animals terrified him. He often thought that they had left him there for good. As he grew older, he became more difficult. When Rodney and Marie returned home from a trip, Ada, who took care of us, would give Budson a bad report. He was difficult, defiant, and disrespectful, she told them, and Rodney would erupt: "So, you've been at it again!" Angry, he would shake Budson and shove him around. Budson seethed. His loyalty in those years was to Andrew, but he looked just like Rodney. There could be no mistaking who his father was.

Roger remembered nothing of his father. He was Ada's darling boy, and when our parents returned and Ada and Joe left, he was inconsolable. He cried himself to sleep, sobbing, "I want Ada," and nothing his mother could do would console him. He was too young when his father died to remember him, but his resemblance to other Salisbury siblings was astonishing. He had the same traits and mannerisms we all had that marked us as Salisburys: curly hair, a great sense of the absurd, and energy. Roger and his mother were estranged from birth, and though they tried to have a loving relationship, or at least to be companionable, it was beyond them. It just never happened, and it was sad for Budson and me to observe. I once said to Roger, "I wish I had a dad," and his quick reply was, "Yah, I wish I had a mother." Once, hearing our mother, drunk, berating Roger in the middle of the night to get up and get wood and kindling, Budson, in frustration, put his fist through the wall. Her youngest child was to bear the brunt of her frustration, anger, and dislike throughout his troubled youth. He learned to fight back with a terrible fury. Once, white-faced with anger, he kicked over the stove in the living room, almost setting the house on fire. One night, I asked her why she didn't like him, as he was smart, beautiful, and sweet. She was playing solitaire and kept moving cards around, not looking up.

It was a bad time when I was pregnant with him, the divorce from Andrew, Rodney trying to get a divorce from Emma—it was the worst time of my life to be pregnant again. The caesarean birth, being in the hospital those months with the infected incision when I nearly died—I just never attached, and he didn't to me, either. I look at him, and he's all the things you say, but I have no motherly impulses of affection for him. He's emotionally a stranger to me, though god knows I try . . . I feel bad, sometimes, and I try.

Then she looked at me. *I've made you sad, Jode. But you have to understand the truth of things. That's not always easy for you.*

I never pass a lumberyard without experiencing a sense of joy. I am on my father's shoulders, hanging on to his nappy hair, while he buys the lumber for my playhouse. It is a girl's fancy, that little house with orange-crate cupboards and a black alphabet on a red table and chairs, and all my dolls in their beds. Then the domestic bliss is shattered when one day, he puts a chicken-wire fence around it with a little gate, and once I am in it, he turns a wooden block that locks it, and he and my mother start to drive away. Panicked, screaming and crying, I crawl that chicken-wire fence like a deranged animal. They start to drive off, and I scream louder until the car slows down, and finally stops. Rodney gets out of the car, unlocks the little gate, and takes me from the fence. Later, because I am suspicious, leery, and won't go into my playhouse, he takes down the fence. He put it there, my mother told me later, in hopes I would not hide in the rumble seat of the car when they were going away on one of their journeys.

A little over a year after Rodney's death, I started the first grade in the fall of 1939 at the North Side School in Billings. It was a strange time, because Marie was sleeping, or she was gone, and I would get up in the morning and dress myself. I had three dresses I was to wear for special occasions only: a bright yellow chiffon, a dark blue taffeta with ruffles, and a silk rose dress with puffed sleeves. Those mornings I dressed myself, I wore one of the forbidden dresses, ate marshmallows, which I loved, and walked to school. I remember sitting in the first grade at a table with a little black girl, and wishing I weren't. She seemed so slow and pitiful, and I didn't want the association. The other kids seemed to ignore her, and me, too. I felt sorry for this pitiful little girl, but I didn't want to be with her. I felt prickly about this, which I now recognize as shame. I knew it wasn't the right way to feel.

I walked the three blocks home from school for lunch, and I remember days when Mom made us special treats of poached eggs in milk and cinnamon toast. One day, she told me that my brother Jim was coming to visit us. I didn't remember him at all, but I was excited that he was coming, and every day, I would hurry home, because I hoped he would be there. One lovely autumn day, there he was. He had just turned fifteen. He was electric, with bright red hair and large purple eyes with long, spider-like lashes. Before I went back to school that day, he bent down, took a little comb out of his shirt pocket, and carefully combed my hair, smoothed my bangs. I was looking right into his eyes, his freckles, his white teeth when he laughed. My big brother—how beautiful!

I don't know how long he stayed with us, but I know he didn't go to school. He would sit on the front stoop and play his trumpet. When he played "I Dream of Jeannie with the Light Brown Hair," that was the signal I was to go to bed. I loved the song, but I hated the reason for it. The Bury girls from across the street would come over and dance to his trumpet. I'd go to sleep, hearing their talk and laughter.

Then he disappeared. He had run away from Andrew and his new wife,

Leora, to see us. One day he was gone, and next we heard he had joined a band in Helena. He was in and out of school, and finally quit to join the Navy when he was seventeen. My mother worried. *He's homeless, doesn't like his father, Andrew, and can't live with him, and hates his stepmother. What will become of him?* I didn't see him again until he left the Navy, when he was twenty-five and I was sixteen, and he came to Arlee to be with us. From that time on, my musically talented, smart, witty brother, Jim, was one of my favorite siblings. Together, it was as if he was the best of his father, and I was the best of our mother, and we forged a common bond. We both went to the University of Montana together and remained friends for the rest of our lives. When he died at the age of ninety-three in Astoria, Oregon, his daughters, Stacy and Andrea, and I organized a celebration of his life, and his friends and ex-music students gave him a loving farewell. They brought their instruments and played, and told stories about him that would have made him laugh.

I listen to jazz, Louis Armstrong, Ella Fitzgerald, Billy Eckstein, and I think of the last time I saw him in Astoria. Sitting on a bench in the spring sun, we were able to say everything that needed saying. He knew he was dying, and he was unafraid.

Later that same fall, my sister Anneva came and stayed with us. At fourteen she seemed sophisticated and mature to me, and very pretty. Mom fussed over her, treated her like a formal guest she wanted to please. This confused me, and I was jealous. Later, I realized that Anneva and our mother were strangers and didn't know each other. There was a stiffness, an unease between them from years of not having lived together and getting to know each other through the informality of family life. It never changed and was a sadness for both of them. I was fascinated by this older sister and was her eager errand girl, going to the store to get her Hershey bars, licorice, and cans of black olives, which she loved. She would lie in the sun reading and eating olives, or sit at the table with a mirror, fixing her hair and painting her nails. She was so grown up. I was fascinated.

That is the only time I remember her visiting us as a girl. Later, she and a friend stopped to see us on their way to Seattle to work in a war plant. She was pretty and animated, excited about this new adventure.

I didn't see her again until she was on her honeymoon, married right out of high school, much to my mother's despair. One particular moment stands out that illustrates their estrangement. My mother and I have gone to Wolf Point to visit Anneva, and as we pull into the driveway, a familiar embroidered linen tablecloth done in shades of rose and gray is on the clothesline catching the wind, dragging in the mud. It is a gorgeous piece of artistry that my mother gave her daughter as a wedding present.

I will say nothing about this, and I don't want you to, either. But I will never again give Anneva any of my hand work. She hasn't developed a taste or appreciation for the time and care behind the work I did here, made especially for her.

Somewhere in this time frame, I have memories of my mother running a little restaurant in Billings called Scotty's. Her partner in this enterprise was Carrie Nugent, whose husband was the editor of the *Billings Gazette* at that time. The restaurant specialized in chili and homemade bread and pies. I remember going there after school and having pie and milk. Sitting there, eating my mother's food in a restaurant, I felt proud that she was the owner. It seemed important. Like so many of her dreams and schemes, it didn't last, though the forty-five pieces of Fiestaware that she purchased for the restaurant were to follow us for years. Mom used to joke that during my turbulent, angry teenage years, I broke so many dishes they dammed up Finley Creek, and it overflowed and almost flooded us out. She thought this was very funny. Those dishes, to me, in all their colorful splendor, were witness to failure. It's funny to say, but she did try to earn a living for us. She could imagine and dream up wonderful schemes of charmed success, but getting those ideas into the real world with persistence and fortitude was fraught with problems. Reality always trumped the dream, and witnessing this in our mother made the three of us more realistic and practical. As we grew older, we rolled our eyes, sneered, and mocked her dreams. We became smart-assed know-it-alls.

A vivid memory I carry with me from Billings is my mother sorting out the house because she is going to fumigate for bedbugs. The boxes of fumigation potion are bright and colorful, like yellow and green cakes with candles. When you lit these candles, you had to leave the house for twenty-four hours, and that included time to air it out to make sure all the fumes were gone, as well as the bedbugs. I remember the boxes of fumigation, how inviting they looked, but I also had this other feeling that they were dangerous. Somehow, I got it into my childish mind that she was going to burn down the house with these boxes of beautiful cakes. This is the story she told me when I was an adult, asking her questions about the past, especially the fire:

Well, it was a hard time, Pet. Rodney's death, facing the uncertain future, I was desperate. I had no money. I wanted to get us out in the country, away from the big-city influences of Billings. It was the only way I could see that we could survive, with a garden, a cow, some chickens. The only thing I owned was the house. Funny, isn't it, that Rodney insisted on that, that the house belong to me, that it was in my name only when we bought it? Good thing, too, because Emma, merciless as she was toward me, would have taken it and left us homeless.

I could see that she was starting to think about Emma, and I knew from experience that bitterness would overwhelm her. It was the same whenever she went into the memory-laden past of her life with Andrew. That house in Billings, I speculate now, was the price Andrew paid to get his children in the divorce settlement. It also represented the children she had given up to be with Rodney, and move to Billings, and buy a home. She was agitated, and at times like this, I used to see her as lost and struggling, surrounded by darkness. I waited; I knew she would return. The power of the story would bring her back, the shaping and telling of it. Reflecting about it now, I think this retelling, over and over, was a form of therapy for her. It was her experiences retold to her artistic satisfaction. She did not make art out of the more sordid elements of her life with Rodney. Those I found out for myself.

That day, I was getting the house ready for fumigation. I moved food and a few clothes, some toys, out to the back house, the house where Ada and Joe used to stay when they worked for us. You remember them? When they left, Roger cried himself to sleep, calling for her. He wouldn't let me near him.

It is an old story, and parts of it, like the colorful boxes of poison and my fear that Mom was going to burn down the house, resonated with me until this day. What I remember most vividly, though, is the fire. We had moved out to the little house in the back where Ada and Joe had lived, and for some reason I remember we had milk toast for dinner, and Budson read comics to Roger and me. We were on an adventure. The next thing I knew, we were awakened by a pounding on the door and excited voices, but what I saw, looking out the window, was the top of our house exploding like a giant volcano into the dark sky. It was beautiful and exciting, and made me happy.

The next image I have of that time is the solitary figure of my mother going through the debris of the burned house, sorting through the rubble. It is still exact in my mind, like an intricate, intimate portrait of grief. It is a heavy gray day with a somber stillness, a captured moment when nothing moves. That portrait, beautiful and distant, has lived in my mind since the day when I was barely seven years old and found it. My mother is a woman bathed in solitude, loneliness, and yes, defeat. She is looking for something precious out of the ashes. I remember hoping she would find it. Today, the metaphor is surprisingly clear.

Many of the things important to her were secreted away in some clandestine place. These objects eventually emerged, and followed us through those chaotic years after Rodney's death, and long after that, too. Baby pictures of Roger and myself, taken in that house with a blue vase, stayed with us through the years, as well as a photo of my father, the one he had taken when he ran for governor of Montana on the Communist ticket. He is handsome, with a high receding forehead, a crown of kinky hair, and calm gray eyes. His presence is a constant in our lives by his very absence. His eyes follow us, immutable in time, powerful, and pervasive. Because he died before we could know him, to us, his youngest children, he is a legendary, romantic figure. We are sure that if he had lived, our lives would be different and better. This is our sour, childish accusation to our mother, who, alive, struggles with raising us. We are not easy children.

There were other vestiges of our father that were hauled from place to place: his finely carved wooden cigar humidor, there on the bookshelf, with stray items on the green velvet lining—bobby pins, pennies, paper clips. We recognized it as a beautiful piece of art, and one day discovered that our mother had given it to him on his fortieth birthday. That was in faraway Plentywood when they were lovers, causing such a stir in that prairie town. Sometimes, I would open it, idly examine it, bring it to my nose and sniff it. It was comforting, the residual smell of my father's cigars.

How my mother was able to save so many things from that fire in Billings, I will never know. I can guess that she took the furniture to the house in the back because of the poisonous fumes those beautiful cakes exuded to kill bedbugs. Perhaps friends also helped her hide precious items away. What I do know is that art and objects from that time ended up far from their originations in Plentywood to a house in Arlee on the Flathead-Salish-Kootenai reservation. Notable in my memory are several pictures of Venice. There is a pair of etchings, water stained, that were always together on a wall, and a large blue painting of Venice that hung over her bed. There was one print, though, that puzzled me when I was a young girl. It was a present from Rodney to Marie when she gave birth to their first child together, my brother Budson. That picture, with the cobalt-blue background, of a partially naked woman, kneeling with her face in her hands, weeping, always intrigued me. It reminded me of my mother and all the spoken and unspoken secrets she could never utter, but only weep away. The picture is, to my mind now, melodramatic and sentimental. I know she liked it, the romantic feeling it conveyed of a woman hurt by love and life. When Rodney gave it to her, did he see her that way? A beautiful woman, with luxurious hair, her hands hiding her many sorrows? Or was it just a feminine portrait he gave to her, another lovely, romantic figure?

Those pictures, as well as my father's library, are here in my house now as I write this. They are all gathered in a room upstairs, and have been in place there for so long, I hardly ever notice them. They are wallpaper from the past. She must have left them with friends, as well as some favorite clothes of hers, and some clothes she had made for Jim and Anneva that eventually were handed down to Roger and me: a sailor suit, and a maroon worsted-wool English riding outfit, complete with the laced-up riding boots. What she had chosen to keep were things important to her, but not necessarily valuable. There were practical, useful things, too. Items of furniture, a table and a medicine chest made by Rodney, and an ornate silver-plated mirror, which lived with us for many years. It was an exquisite mirror, framed in old silver with a curved, beveled center and an ornate, slim panel framing it on each side. It glowed in all its tarnished splendor in our shabby little living room on the reservation.

Not too much later she sold the Billings land, and from then on, 901 North 22 Street was a magical number, remembered by my two brothers and me as the turbulent times in Billings after our father died. Many years later, my husband, Vern, and our daughter, Allison, were in Billings and looked up this address. The neighborhood I remembered was gone. It was now a part of industrial Billings, though I did find along a fence several small rose bushes, and I fancied they were probably planted by my mother. The big old cotton-wood tree was still in the boulevard in front of the house. It brought to mind an image of going to find my mother on a summer day when we lived at that address. I find her in the garden. She is a small figure in bibbed overalls with her wild copper hair escaping from her straw hat. She is directing little rows of water down a canal to water the garden. It must be late summer, because I stand at the end of the garden awash in the golden light of early morning. When she sees me, wordlessly, she washes a tomato in the irrigation ditch and holds it up to see if I want it. I nod, and walk toward her and take the voluptuous red orb from her hand. It is warm from the sun, mealy, deli-cious. She feeds me that morning a radish, a carrot, shelled peas. There is a serene feeling to this tableau. It is a singular, memorable event in light of the troubled times ahead.

Looking back on our lives in Billings after my father's death, I can only see a life in shambles, totally at the whim of whether our mother was drinking, hung over, or sober. I was often sick with colds, tonsillitis, earaches, and as a result, was hearing impaired. When my mother, restless and lonely, went on one of her endless journeys for whatever mysterious reason, she would often take me with her. I missed a lot of school, but I remember a lovely young girl coming to our house and giving me dancing lessons in the living room. At some point, I was taken to see Dr. Morledge in Billings, and he recommended I have my tonsils and adenoids removed. My mother created an air of excitement and celebration about the coming hospital event so I would not be frightened. That all faded when I woke up from the ether, sick to my stomach, thinking of death. There was the stillness of the winter light coming in the window of my hospital room. Alone, I wondered if I would ever be well again and be home with my brothers. I was seven years old.

We are in a state of flux, moving from place to place. We leave Billings, and Marie buys three houses in Butte on the flats. She is gone, we don't know where. She leaves us with people we don't know. I wake up in a dark room to wild yelling and screaming, the noise of falling, crashing objects. A voice yells, "Down with the meat house!" and there is a booming crash. A voice, I recognize it as my mother's, says calmly, "You're all right, Gaylord . . . easy, easy, now." I hear the sirens, see the flashing lights. The police. I lie in the dark, shivering. I see a flash of light as the door opens and Budson comes in. He brings a glass of water, makes me drink, then crawls in bed with me, tells me a story.

Another time, we are staying with the Clines, whose son Lennie is a friend of our mother's. There are rumors that the Clines are thieves, and Lennie is in and out of prison. I remember that he is handsome, with shiny Brylcreem hair and smelling of cologne. He and our mother sit at the table talking and sometimes get in the car and leave. It is Christmastime, and Mrs. Cline, Lennie's mother, makes taffy and gives us sweet, buttery spoonfuls. They have a flock of turkeys, and sometimes I go in their yard and wander around until a big bird chases me, nipping at me as I run, terrified. We sleep in a dark room with musty old blankets. I wear the same dress to school, dull and limp, and my lunch box is redolent of baloney and stale food. Sometimes we are locked in our room, and they leave. We stand at the window, longing to be outside playing in the sun, until twilight falls and the sun disappears. Budson is nervous, desperate, too quiet. He has searched the room for a window that might open. He mostly stands by the window, his arm leaning into the frame, resting his head in his hand. He looks sad and defeated. What if our mother never comes back? We know what it feels like to be orphans, with nobody caring.

It happens! Our mother returns and takes us away. We fall on her with cries of joy and later regale her with stories about the Clines. *I paid them well to take care of you, and they promised. What frauds! They turned into sweaty-palmed capitalists at the smell of money! Never again will I trust them with my children, never again.*

We are in a strange house in Butte. There is no furniture, and it is dark outside and shadowed and quiet inside. I am in a corner with a blanket spread on the floor. My doll, teddy bear, and books are lined up neatly. I have lemon drops and a small package of figs. What I see is my mother sitting at a small table in the center of the empty room. The only light is from the small lamp on the table. She is bent over a book, her arm resting on the table, her head in her hand, reading.

She calls to me. *Will you come here, please?*

I walk over to the circle of light and stand next to her. She puts her arm around my waist, and brings me closer. *Will you help me?* she asks. That's all I remember.

It is a cold winter in Butte. The windows are frosted over, and water freezes on the floor. The schools are closed. Whooping cough, scarlet fever, diphtheria scour the neighborhood. Bright red and yellow "Quarantined" signs appear on the doors and windows of houses. We have a woodstove going full blast, and the teakettle whistles. The oven door is open to warm the kitchen. "Careful, now . . ." I hit it with my knee, and the burn becomes infected. Before we go to bed, our mother makes us eat half a sandwich of sliced raw garlic on buttered brown bread. She squeezes lemons and mixes the juice with honey, and we take spoonfuls, like cough medicine. We gargle with saltwater. We wash our hands with Fels Naptha soap.

To keep warm, my two brothers and I sleep in one big room off of the kitchen. Budson has a regular bed, and Roger and I have a small cot next to him. We are in bed early, hearing the murmur of distant voices. Budson sneaks in and whispers, loud enough for us to hear: "The boogey man is here, and he's going to take you two little choice morsels away, right now, and chew on your tender bones." We scream with excitement and mock terror. He leaves, and we wait. Then we call to him, "Hey Mr. Boogeyman, come in here. We're not afraid of you!" We wait, giggling. Just as we are about to doze off, he bursts through the door, snarling and growling, "Who are those silly little creatures who say they are not afraid? Say it now, now." He wrings his hands, and looms over us. We are hysterical with glee, screaming and laughing.

We wake to smoke, see flames coming from the kitchen, angry voices, Budson and our mother. Budson pulls us out of the room on our blankets, drags us to the front door, and puts us in the trundle seat of the car. Smoke and flames are pouring out of the windows of the house. Budson is at the wheel; our mother is sitting next to him. "Go!" she says. "Go!" Roger and I join in the chorus.

The engine gives a dull, churning sound. It won't turn over. He tries again and again. The fire is looming closer. Finally, with much heaving and jerking, we are moving . . . moving. Looking back, I see that the house is enveloped in smoke, and flames are licking out the windows.

Our mother and Budson are gone. Roger and I have been left with Carrie and Monte Nugent, her good friends. Like Marie, Monte is a newspaper person and works for the *Billings Gazette*. Before Rodney died, the two couples were friends. Monte and Carrie live in a fairy-tale house of gold stucco with colorful petunias in the window boxes. A narrow brick walk meanders to the three front steps. They are a half-circle, topped by a sturdy carved door. Inside, the hardwood floors gleam, and Rags, their dog, slumbers by the fireplace. Monte smokes a pipe, and when he is home he is always reading—the paper, books, letters. If we are nearby, he will put out his arms, and we are encircled, each on one side of him. He reads to us, commenting on the news. We listen to the sound of his voice, feeling safe in his circle, though we don't know the meaning of what he reads. Carrie smells of perfume when she hugs us; her short, curly blonde hair is pulled back by a bright ribbon. "People think you are my kids," she says, laughing.

The kitchen is the brightest spot in the house. The sun pours in the windows, and we are bathed in its golden light as we eat pancakes, or bacon and eggs, or waffles. There is a clothes chute from the kitchen down to the basement, and Roger is at one end, I am at the other. I throw a ball down, and he tries to throw it back. It skitters crazily, making a hollow sound on the sides of the tin chute. Carrie laughs.

She is sewing, and she calls me over to try on another dress. "You'll be in the second grade, just think, and you've grown out of all of your clothes! In August, you'll be eight years old! There will be Indian children in your class. Isn't that exciting?"

But it is our bedroom upstairs that is truly magical. Carrie's mother lived in it before she died. We imagine her ghost is there, a friendly presence. There is a large dresser, and one drawer is for our clothes. Exploring, we open another drawer, and find lacy blue and pink nightgowns with matching bed jackets carefully folded in their boxes. We each don one of the fancy bed jackets and dance, whirling around until we are dizzy, and laughing, we collapse on the floor. We find silk stockings, boxes of delicate handkerchiefs. In another drawer we find boxes of stationary, some still in their wrappings, an opened box with the initials, AMA. Surprised and excited, at the bottom of the drawer, we find boxes of unopened beribboned chocolates! We dare to open one. The candy is frosted, white with age. We each take one. We are happy discoverers.

The first letter I ever received was that summer we lived with Carrie and Monte. It was from Budson. "He addressed it so sweet!" Carrie says. "To my little sister, Jo Anne." In this letter, Budson tells me that we have a farm on the Flathead Reservation at Arlee. There are Indians living in teepees, he says, and kids ride their horses to school. "There is a big straw stack that you can slide down, and eighty acres to walk around in. The school bus runs right past our house, and we'll ride it to school." I am excited. Indians in feather headdresses and moccasins at school! Teepees! Bows and arrows!

It is late summer when we leave Monte and Carrie Nugent's house in Billings. Carrie is driving and Monte is smoking and reading. With the smoke from his pipe, the hot sun through the window, the swaying of the car, I am nauseated. Carrie has made a big picnic lunch, and somewhere out of Helena by the hot springs, we settle on the grass and eat cold chicken, potato salad, and gingerbread. Carrie and Monte tell us how many miles to go, how much more time, but it only means we are getting closer to Arlee, the promised land. Back in the car, I nap.

We are home. Our mother cries, hugs us, but we are soon off with Budson to find the straw stack. Though we try and try to climb its slippery slopes, we always slide back and can never reach the highest point. Taking each one of us by a hand, Budson tries to pull us up to the top. We slip and slide. The straw gets under our shirts. We itch. Laughing, we all tumble down together. We explore the machine shed, the outhouse (three holes!), the chicken coop, the rabbit hutches, but it is the storage house, sturdy and squat, that intrigues me. It has a heavy door, hard to open. We all pull on it, and our success is the fruity smell of McIntosh apples. Budson polishes several on his sleeve, and at the first bite into the crisp juicy apple, they become my favorites forever.

Later, Carrie brings out a surprise chocolate cake that she had baked before we left Billings. It is in a pretty box, and when she removes the cake, we are surprised. It is covered with popcorn. She and my mother laugh. "It's to keep the cake from falling apart," Carrie says. "It's for a surprise birthday party for Budson and Jo Anne, September and August." It was my eighth birthday in August, Budson's thirteenth in September.

Soon after the party, Carrie and Monte get ready to leave. As they pack up their car, Carrie is crying. For a moment, I remember the feeling of wanting to get back in the car and go with them. Roger hesitates, too. My mother told me, many years later:

You two stood there, hugging Carrie who was carrying on and crying, each of you taking one of Monte's hands, wanting, I really think, to get in the car, and leave with them. You looked at them, you looked at me, and then Budson took you both by the hand, and walked away with you; but still, you both looked back. Carrie wanted you for her children, I could tell. Her voice drifted off. She was having a melancholy mood. Maybe—it would have been better?

"No, Mom," I assured her. "We already had a family."

38

I'm sitting here, writing this memoir of my father and mother, Rodney Salisbury and Marie Chapman Hansen, trying to get to the heart of these two people who lived in their interesting times, the volatile twentieth century. I think of the English writer and biographer, Penelope Lively, and can totally recognize in myself what she is saying: "The memory we live with—the form of memory that most interests me—is the moth-eaten version of our own past that each of us carries around, depends on. It is our ID; this is how we know who we are and where we have been."[23]

ARLEE

Indelible memory takes me back to that autumn of 1941, living on the reservation at Arlee in that small, one-bedroom house, walking down the driveway in the mellow autumn sunshine with my two brothers to catch the bus to school. I was in the second grade, Roger in the first grade, and Budson, because he had skipped two grades, was the youngest and smallest freshman in high school.

Where did my expectations come from, the ones where the school on the reservation would have Indian children who rode horses to school and wore moccasins, leather clothes, and feather headdresses? So much of my eagerness about going to the second grade was this happy thought, and I even went so far as to imagine my best friend would be an Indian princess.

The reality I faced in that classroom was a puzzle to me. Coming through the door, I saw three large desks against the wall. They belonged to three boys, "breeds" as they were called, who had repeatedly failed the first and second grades. Now, at least ten, maybe eleven years old, they were trying school once again. The rest of the kids looked like me. I left school that first day and didn't wait for the bus, but ran all the way home. "Where are the Indian kids? They are not in the school, not anywhere. What happened to them?"

My next anxious question was, "Why don't I know how to write? Everyone else can write, but me. Show me, right now . . . now!"

I was eight years old in the second grade, and I could not write cursive. I was still doing baby printing, with large, clumsy letters. My mother carefully and clearly wrote down a Shakespearean sonnet, and I mindlessly copied her written letters, "Shall I compare thee to a summer's day?" I eventually learned to write, and somewhere in the process memorized sonnet XVIII, which, like a parrot, I could recite but had no sense of its meaning.

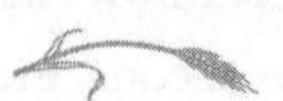

39

We were not prepared for the bleak, uninterrupted cold that assailed us that first winter in Arlee. Our mother soon became a regular at the two local bars, the Log Cabin and the Stockman. Often, when she was sick and hung over, Budson would get us up on those cold winter mornings, build a fire, and make pancakes for us. He would serve us each one pancake at a time, and we'd eat around the outer edge, because though they were burned, they were raw in the center, runny and cold. Years later, it was one of our favorite jokes: "Hey, Budson, how about some of those great Arlee pancakes?" He'd laugh, and tell us, "You have to have a woodstove and especially green wood that burns a cold fire to get a great pancake like that."

As the winter wore on, the pump froze, and we'd melt snow for water. But later, there was no snow and we couldn't thaw the pump. Budson, by this time, had a good friend named Bud McMurtrie, who lived in town. Bud came from a family with a lot of kids, and they were friendly and resourceful. When Budson showed up on their doorstep asking for water, they loaned him a cart and put two barrels of water on it. Budson and Bud splashed up the road to our house, at least a mile away. Several times that winter Budson would go there for water so we could bathe, wash clothes, and have drinking water. On those dark winter nights after school, the bitter wind in his face, he would push the cart with the two barrels of splashing water up the highway to our house.

Stepping off the school bus at the end of a bleak winter day, we would stand for a minute and watch the chimney. If there was smoke lazily drifting out of it, we knew she was home, and maybe hot soup, freshly baked bread, and cookies or an apple pie would be waiting for us. If the chimney was still, unresponsive, we knew we had to build a fire, find something to eat, do our homework, and wait for her to show up.

Roger and I began to notice that when we got on the bus, Budson would go directly to the back and sit with this pretty girl named Donna Pearson. They would hold hands and lean their heads in close and talk in whispers. She had blonde hair, full red lips, a small waist cinched in with a belt, and round hips. She wore little plastic flower earrings and was a cheerleader. Roger and I and other kids on the bus would sing, a parody, "Donna, I'm in love with you, Donna, with your eyes so blue." It was annoying and embarrassing to Budson, but Donna just laughed. Budson was so smitten. He would earnestly talk to Roger and me, asking us not to start singing the song, and we'd promise. But as soon as we got on the bus and he hurried back to Donna, we couldn't help ourselves. We'd start singing "Donna, with your eyes so blue," and everyone would chime in, laughing and carrying on until Bill Siphers, the bus driver, threatened to stop the bus and cast us out in the cold to walk the rest of the way to school. He wasn't joking, either. He meant it.

Sometimes, those evenings when we were all alone doing our homework, Budson would get up and tell us he'd be back in an hour. From our house to Donna's was at least a mile, and on those winter evenings he would jog to her house, stand in the moonlight, and look at her lighted window. He didn't knock, or go in to see her. He just stood there in the moonlight, and when the light in her window went dark, shivering in his light jacket, he would turn and run back to us.

One evening we got off the bus, and there was smoke coming from the chimney. Our mother was home. We hurried to the house, and when we entered the back door, we could smell the delicious sugar and cinnamon of a McIntosh apple pie. By now the apples were shriveled, but they still made good applesauce and pies. There was the yeasty smell of bread ready to come out of the oven, and chili simmering on the back of the stove. The table was set with a tablecloth, napkins, and fancy plates. We were excited and, as always, hungry.

Our mother was looking weary, hung over, but now there were times when she stayed sober, maybe for a few weeks, cleaning the house from "garret to cellar," as she would say, moving furniture around, even painting. We were always willing to believe this was one of those times, always hoping our lives would be more like those of our friends, with stable mealtimes, our clothes washed and ironed, the house warm and inviting. Like the McMurtries.

The formality of this time, the table setting, the food, our mother's solemn air, was to mark a date in our memories forever: December 7, 1941. The Japanese had bombed Pearl Harbor. As we gathered around the table, eating, asking questions, our mother expressed her great sorrow that young boys would be fighting and dying in this senseless war.

If it lasts a long time, Jim could be called to active duty, or you, Budson. And Rodney's sons, Mike and Eugene, they will be called to fight this capitalists' war. Money will be made by the powerful profiteers of guns and bombs, munitions. It's just a way to bring us out of the depression, a war economy. So many boys will die or be maimed forever for grandiose words, like patriotism, freedom, the red, white, and blue. Such a waste! Let us hope it will be of short duration.

Later that night, we listened on our battery radio to President Roosevelt talking about the war in calm, measured tones, but with a sense of urgency, too. Overnight, the world had changed. I remember Budson saying that Prof Wittwer, principal of the Arlee school, had written on the board that day a quote from President Roosevelt, and wanted each student to write it down in their notebooks: "Yesterday, December 7, 1941—a date that will live in infamy—the United States of America was suddenly and deliberately attacked by naval and air forces of the empire of Japan."

For the three of us, the world had turned ominous. The war was far away, but as close as our radio. The commenters, with their blow-by-blow descriptions and analysis of what was happening, gave the war an eerie reality. I remember the sense of wonder and awe while I practiced cursive writing, copying the sonnet. I found it years later, my childish scrawl, tucked in a book, dated December 8, 1941, one day after Pearl Harbor.

Sometime after the war started, two strange men in dark suits showed up at our door, and our mother stood outside, talking to them while they took notes. After they left, she was visibly shaken. She stayed sober for several weeks, sad and worried, writing letters to Wolf Point and Plentywood, which I mailed at the post office before I took the bus home. Later we learned the men were from the government, the FBI, checking on her activities, what organizations she belonged to, her political leanings. Several times during the war they returned. They were keeping a file on her.

Our first Christmas in Arlee, our mother left for town on Christmas Eve day to get the mail, but after so much time passed, we knew she had stopped at the Log Cabin bar. We had been watching for her out the window, and finally she appeared out of the falling snow with a quart of beer under each arm, singing "Loch Lomond." She could turn angry, too, and lash out if we scorned her drunken state. How sharper than a serpent's tooth it is to have a thankless child! was one of her favorite Shakespearean quotes. She could be bellicose and insulting, but before the evening was over, she was crying, telling us about her two children, Jim and Anneva, who were not with us. Through the many years and many Christmases, any celebration could be interrupted by her memory of this loss, and she would disappear into her inconsolable grief. We were outside looking in, knowing there was something about these absent children that was important to her, maybe more than we were, so always present, so needy.

Then ordinary tasks would swallow up the time, and she seemed to forget about them, and we did, too.

That Christmas we had a tree that Budson got in the hills surrounding Arlee. The three of us decorated it with strings of popcorn, cranberries, and red and green colored loops. Somehow our mother managed to get us presents. My brothers got bows and arrows and Woolrich plaid jackets. During those sober days, she crocheted scarves as presents for all of us, which we had for years. But most surprising of all, Budson returned from the post office with two large packages. They were from Butte, Montana. In one package there were three Christmas stockings, one for each of us, with an orange, a delicious apple, ribbon candy, and some unshelled nuts. At the bottom of the package, there was a shoebox with pieces of cake and some cookies. The other package was a present for me: a small wooden box with a lock and key. Inside were some ribbons and a pair of pajamas. There was a blue sweater for our mother and an envelope.

These are gifts from an old friend of your father's. He's a Catholic Irishman, a great storyteller, and a union man. He so liked and admired your father that when Rodney died, he wanted to help. It's here, in this envelope.

This was the first we knew of him. His name was Ed Lawler, and the hundred dollars he sent every month made it possible for us to survive.

Dreams and plans often enlarged her vision beyond the bleak present. She had marvelous schemes of how we could succeed. One of her favorite plans was to open a restaurant. Her cooking talents took her in this direction, as we know from The People's Bakery that she and Rodney had in Plentywood, and Scotty's, the one she started with Carrie later in Billings after Rodney died. She loved to cook and to feed people. Hung-over, flailing her way to sobriety, she would bake caramel rolls, scalloped potatoes, Southern fried chicken. The house, redolent with tantalizing smells, was always a sign to us that she was on the mend. Her culinary skills were always talked about in grandiose terms. Rich, beautiful food, tempting the most indifferent palate, was her gift.

Here we are, this house by the side of the road, right by that Highway 93 out there, people going by all day long. We could serve Sunday chicken dinners, you know, fried chicken, mashed potatoes, creamed peas, and apple pie, real home-cooked food. People would come from Missoula just to have a good meal. We'd have a carpenter come and build a room off the front room, and that would be our restaurant . . . or just to begin, we could have a couple of tables set up in the living room, and seat people that way. The couches you boys sleep on could just be couches, you know? Budson, you could be the waiter, wear a jacket and tie, and greet people, and Jody, you could clear and set the tables, make them look nice with flowers, and wear a pretty dress, and Roger could help wash dishes, and play the harmonica, or recite a poem.

Though we knew better even as young as we were, the three of us would listen enthralled, caught up in her dream. We would add our ideas, like having real linen tablecloths and napkins, several pies to choose from, and strawberry shortcake in season, and she would share our excitement. In those moments, it seemed our success as a unified, working family was guaranteed. Then the mystical moment would drift off into the press of the real world, the world of poverty, bills, hard work, and loss. Always, there was the sense of loss.

Why we left this place by the side of the road after that one winter had something to do with too little money, too much land for us to care for, too little water, too far from town without a car. The man who owned the place showed up as we were packing up to leave. Years later, Budson, an actor and tale spinner, as well as a successful businessman, would entertain Roger and me with this story:

"We were just packing up the furniture and putting it on this flatbed truck that the McMurtries loaned us when Mr. Pritchet showed up to take a look at the place before we left. 'You owe me two months rent, but I ain't figuring on getting a cent of that.' He sort of shuffled around, spit a couple of times, took a chew. But what I'd like to know, Budson, is what happened to the goddamned machine shed? Actually, there ain't no shed. There's the rake, the old tractor, just sittin' there pretty as you please, out in the god-damn open, just waiting for the snow and rain to rust it up real good. So where's the goddamn shed, kid, just tell me straight on.'

"Mr. Pritchet, I said, I tore the shed down during the winter, and used it for firewood to keep us warm. My little sister was sick with the chicken pox. The wood we got from your brother was green, and burned a cold fire."

"About that time, you and Roger came over and stood beside me. You both knew I was in trouble. Do you remember that? You, Jo Anne, came up behind me and put your arms around my waist and just hung on. You were scared. Mr. Pritchet continued, 'Goddamest thing I've ever heard. You tore down my machine shed, and burned it up, have I got this right?'

"Yes, Mr. Pritchet. You've got that right. Really sorry, but it was so cold . . ."

"'Yeh, I know, I know. And where was your Ma while all this tearing and burning was going on? Was she just watching you, or was it her idea? Goddamn!' And he spit again."

"Then the strangest thing happened." Here Budson leaned back in his chair, smiling a little, in one of his thoughtful reveries that we knew so well. "He looked at the three of us, saw our poorness, saw your little hands, Jo Anne, holding on to my waist, and you, Roger, hands in your back pockets, head down, scuffling the ground with your foot, shy, embarrassed. Then Mr. Pritchet took off his hat, scratched his head, peered at us, and started to laugh. First, his belly shook, and then he laughed harder and harder, slapping his hat against his leg, and staggered over to his pick-up, got in, and as he turned to leave bent down to where the three of us were standing, and said, 'I got a job for you, Budson. Three dollars a day. I'll be by.'"

42

I claim experiences that are banked in my memory to this day from the time I was eight years old. All my senses were alert to this new place we had moved to in town, and where we would live for many years. How can I describe the shack that was our new home, there in that spot close to the railroad tracks? The house was four walls with no foundation, just slabs of wood crisscrossed on two-by-fours, and the dampness seeped up through the floorboards and invaded the rooms. All the years we lived in that house, there was the insidious smell of mold and decay, as if the house had been abandoned through many seasons and still was. The closet was the only room that was finished, and the inside was covered with old newspapers from the early 1900s. In the rest of the house, there were studs indicating rooms. We walked from space to space, passing through permeable walls, figuring out there were two bedrooms, a living room, and a kitchen because there was a cookstove there. Meanwhile, our mother disappeared. We were never surprised, her leaving without a word to us, and we carried on, Budson telling Roger and me which boxes to empty and where to put the contents. As the day darkened, we lit the lamps, the acrid smell of kerosene assailed us, and the light threw our shadows in grotesque forms on the ceiling and studs. When I think of that scene now, I see us held together by our remarkable resiliency, our sense that if we did it right, put things together in the proper order, we would hold our world together. We listened to our older brother and learned to figure things out.

Later, we got a fire going and, sitting on the mattresses on the floor, ate peanut butter on crackers for our supper.

"What are we doing here?" I asked Budson.

"Camping out,"

"We're going to start a restaurant," Roger said, "serve Sunday dinners. See how easy it will be? No walls to slow us up."

We lay back on the beds, helpless with laughter.

Sometime in the night, our mother returned and was with us when we woke up in terror, the house trembling as if the walls would crumble, our beds vibrating. There was a roaring in our ears, and a large beam of light illuminated the spaces between the studs. There she was, smelling of whiskey, standing over us.

It's just the 4:00 o'clock troop train. It's slowing down for the depot to get water. Pretty soon, you won't notice it any more and will sleep through it. There's a moon tonight. Let's go outside and see it. You'll like this place, just wait and see. It has a stand of trees, a little forest, and a creek runs through our ten acres. You can fish. We can raise an acre of garlic and make a good living. And so another dream began and ended.

We didn't know it then, but the train and its destinations to other parts of the world became fixed in our imaginations. The world extended beyond this place, this bit of time. On the other side of the house was Finley Creek, which ran through our land. The two points of departure were parentheses around our lives for all the time we lived in Arlee. Finley Creek was a constant source of adventure for all three of us and our friends. We all fished, and many times the fish we caught were our supper, those little firm brook trout. On summer days and weekends, Roger and I got up early and, with a can of worms and our handmade fishing poles, headed for the creek and our favorite spots for catching those wily little trout. At the end of our favorite fishing holes was a flat, open space where we had stashed a sack of salted flour, some butter, and a frying pan. We gathered sticks, built a fire, cleaned our fish, and tossed them in the frying pan, where they curled up, they were so fresh. We ate whatever we caught for our breakfast, cleaned the pan, put out the fire, stashed the sack of flour, and searched the pasture for our horses. We spent those summer days roaming the hills and valleys of Arlee on horseback, swimming and wading in Finley Creek, and only hunger and our chores drove us back to that little house by the tracks and our mother. In later years, I would reflect that being neglected most of the time and left to our own minds and imaginations gave us the freedom to explore the hills and valleys of Arlee. It left an indelible mark on us. We absorbed its many seasons into our psyches, and never tired of its ever-changing beauty. On mellow autumn nights, memory takes me back to Arlee, and wandering the countryside with Roger and our friends. The harvest moon is low, and we are transfixed in its golden light. We go to Hughie's house, and throw small stones on his basement bedroom window, and he sneaks out to join us. Hungry, we dig potatoes and find corn left from the harvest. We dig a hole, put rocks in the bottom, then the potatoes and unshucked corn, more rocks, and build a fire on top. While it cooks, we sit on the bank of Finley Creek singing and joking, sometimes quietly talking. The corn is tender, the potatoes perfect. We are awed by our own youth, and the possibilities that lie ahead. We cannot find our way home until the moon falls away, the stars fade, and a smear of light appears in the east. Then we walk out of the sacred circle, into the light of a new day, into our future.

For our mother, this little farm harkened back to a romanticized, miniature version of life on the ranch in Plentywood. She raised a large kitchen garden on the rich loamy soil, both beautiful and abundant. After these many years, her reveries about seeds and their miraculous nature linger with me still.

Just imagine, Pet, this little seed can live in a sack in the cupboard for years, but given the proper soil and water and careful attention, it can grow into a nourishing plant, and produce seeds of its own. It's a miracle, isn't it? A seed is a poem, a painting, a symphony. Do you see?

Extravagance was her answer to nature's abundance. She might plant a quarter of an acre of gladiola bulbs in every hue and color, transplant a large patch of iris, decide on climbing roses in addition to her regular flowers in their wild array of temperament and colors. The first three springs we lived in town, she was so focused on the garden, that drunk, sober, or hung over, no matter how inclement the weather, she would be outside, hauling, digging, planting, weeding, with Roger helping, taking her orders. When she discovered DDT, Roger was enlisted to spray plants, and they flourished even more. As a result of her intemperate gardening sprees, she would catch a cold, and it would turn into pneumonia. Coughing, feverish, struggling to breathe, we would fetch one of the neighbors, and they would take her to St. Pat's hospital in Missoula. One year, she almost died, and suddenly we had a visit from her brother Colie and sister Eva, and Eva's husband, Mac. She had wired them from the hospital. They bought us groceries and stayed with us until she was safe. Her last hospital visit, when again she almost died, there was penicillin and she survived. The three of us understood from our precarious life with our unstable mother that we might be left alone, or that the welfare people might take us away. Survival was ingrained in us, as well as the firmly rooted idea that we would not be separated.

Living in town, we had a more intense experience of reservation life. Across the road from us lived John and Agnes Pellco. John was tall and slim with a long braid that hung halfway down his back. Agnes was round and ample and wore layered, colorful clothes. She always had a bright rose-bedecked bandana around her head, tied in the back, with her braids hanging from each shoulder. John and Agnes were handsome, with white smiles, good humor, and an innate dignity. They walked with measured steps going to and from town, where I would often meet them. Rumors abounded that the sweat lodge they held at their place on Finley Creek had wild, violent doings. An uncommon lot of people died or disappeared mysteriously during the sweat lodge, and drunken revelry was the order of the night. We didn't know any of this, though, when we first became their neighbors. One evening soon after we arrived, there was a knock on the door, and John Pellco had a large sack of venison that he gave our mother. "Just cook it like meat," he said. From time to time, he would show up with more venison or elk. My mother would give him some money and always say, *So, do I cook this like meat, John?* and he would show his white teeth, laugh, and nod.

Now that we lived on the reservation, she had much to say about the Indians, an ongoing conversation she was to have for all the years we lived in the valley. *All the businesses are run by white men, those sizzerbills. They cheat the Indians by selling them over-priced booze, which they can't buy themselves. They can't even sell their land, though it's supposed to belong to them; of course, all this land belongs to them. Many of them hand over their government checks to the local store, trusting souls, where they are cheated month after month. Imagine, a whole way of life for them is gone, all giving way to the white man's greed!*

And so the conversation would go, with variations on a theme. We were definitely a pro-Indian family, unlike a lot of other families in the valley, and we had reason to be.

One day that first summer, we saw John Pellco riding a horse up the driveway to our house. The three of us were always happy to see John, and we walked out to meet him. John slipped off the horse and gave the reigns to Roger. "This is your horse. His name is Buck. He's old, but he's a good horse."

The way Budson told it years later, he offered to take John back to his house on Buck, but John said, "No, I'll walk. That's part of the gift."

Buck's backbone was two inches high, and when he cantered, we became painfully aware of how old and bony he was. We never had a saddle, but we learned to ride him by jostling from cheek to cheek to avoid being split by his prominent backbone. Buck belonged to Roger, and was the first of the many horses he loved and rode in rodeos and races held at the ranches in Arlee. He was an excellent horseman, a fluid rider.

Up the road from us, in the foothills of the mountains that flanked our place, lived Joe Grandjo, one of the chiefs of the Flathead/Salish/Kootenai tribes. On those nights when he held a tribal council, we could hear the drumming as we drifted off to sleep. As if in response to the drumming, the coyotes would howl their lonesome, mournful calls. There was a music, a peaceful center lodged out there in the world, and we were a part of it. Our personal troubles were absorbed in this larger, mysterious cosmos. The stars were thick in the dark sky, and close. Stand tall, and you could touch them.

44

Arlee in 1941 harkened back to the beginnings of this country. Only Main Street and two blocks on each side had electricity. The population was two hundred people, mostly self-subsistence farmers, but some had jobs in Missoula for cash flow. Many of those farmers still plowed with horses. The town had a post office, and in the spring, crates of baby chicks were delivered there, chirping, waiting for someone to pick them up. There were two stores, the Farmers Union, with farming equipment and seeds, and Demer's Mercantile, a grocery store that also sold shoes and clothes. The two-story Arlee Hotel was owned by the corpulent Mrs. Memory, who sat stolidly in her rocking chair by the one window, fixed in time, never venturing out. One of the eeriest events of my young life was the one night my mother and I, for some unremembered reason, stayed in that hotel. The atmosphere was primeval, like a cave, with its one dim light-bulb hanging from the ceiling. The heavy, dark blankets on the lumpy bed smelled of the many unwashed bodies before us. There was a chamber pot by the bed, a washstand in the corner with a basin and a pitcher of water. Down the hall, a party was going on. I could hear the plaintive tunes of a harmonica, and felt safe enough to drift off to sleep.

Behind the hotel there was a bustling blacksmith shop. Two bars dominated the entertainment scene, and our mother had running charge accounts at both—the Log Cabin Bar and Restaurant and the Stockman. Saturdays, most people came to town to get their mail, buy groceries at Demer's, and have a beer at one of the bars. People like my mother often wandered from one bar to the other, lonesome for people and conversation. The owner of the Stockman bar was from Scobey in eastern Montana, and she liked that connection with her beloved prairie. Many mornings she walked to school with us as far as the Log Cabin, stopped there, and began drinking. Returning home after school, she might still be there, or home in bed, drunk, or out in the country at someone's ranch, partying. It was not unusual for her to get in a discussion about politics, and when an opinion differed from her own, to fly into a rage. We were talked about in the village because of her drinking, her impetuous nature, and once two women commented, within hearing distance of us, that Roger and I looked clean despite our mother being a drunk. The books, radical magazines, and papers like the *Militant* that came to us through the post office caused the postmaster to say to me, "You people believe in Christmas?"

We were ever conscious that the war, those four years, was all around us by the troop trains that passed so close to our house every day. We lived about half a block from the depot where the trains stopped for water and to pick up and drop off passengers. It was Pat O'Brian, the depot agent, with his ticker tape, who delivered the missing in action or death notices to the Arlee families. When we saw his black Cadillac churning up dust on Arlee roads, we felt the press of mortality and wondered who was going to get the bad news. Noticing a group of people gathered at the depot, Roger and I would hurry down to see who was leaving for the service, or who was returning. Sometimes, a soldier was on leave, happily greeted by his parents; other times, it was a wounded soldier, surrounded by anxious, concerned family members. Our mother, watching soldiers coming and going, would say, *Poor boys! Deluded by grand words like freedom, liberty, justice, and not even knowing where they are going or why. These capitalist wars are a scourge on our country, and the war machine of death will put money in the coffers of the rich.* About rationing she had much the same to say. *It's an artificial deprivation, wanting us all to buy into the war effort, just propaganda.*

But where we felt the deprivations of the war the most was in the schools. It was difficult to recruit teachers to such a small, uninteresting town, but a few adventurous women from the East tried their luck. All of us that were in that combined third and fourth grade remember in detail Miss Blazovich, a woman as harsh as her name. She often became red-faced with anger at some student's incorrect answer or straying attention, and she would take out a three-sided stick and whack and chase the howling student as they jumped from desk to desk trying to escape her. While we were planning a Christmas party, she threatened that if any of us spoke out of turn, we would get whacked, and the next person would get that doubled. Excited, I had an idea and yelled it out of turn, and got two whacks. When Roger protested, "Leave my sister alone," he got four whacks. Seeing his frail little form bending under the force of her muscled arm, I protested. While Miss Blazovich was giving me the promised eight whacks, I looked at him, and shaking my head, desperately mouthed, "No!"

When we told our mother, she was incensed. We begged her not to do anything, fearing the situation would be worse for us. *This is not what education is about. She is a barbarian of the worst kind, and knows nothing about children and learning. Why do they hire these philistines, anyway? Surely there are some warm bodies out there with a brain or two?*

One afternoon soon after this, just before school was to let out, we heard a knock on the classroom door. Miss Blazovich opened the door to find the principal and a woman standing there. We heard the distinctive, dignified dulcet tones of our sober mother saying, *Miss Blazovich? I am the mother of Jo Anne and Roger. I want to tell you, once and for all, that if you ever lay a hand on my children, or any child in this classroom, I will take it to the highest court in the land, and you will rot in jail. You are, Madame, a shameful excuse for an educator, and I speak not only for myself, but for all the concerned parents of these children.*

We could see the red rising on the back of Miss Blazovich's neck. On hearing this, the children in that classroom, including Roger and me, let out a great yell of triumphant joy. When the bell for dismissal rang, we ran cheering from the room.

We didn't know it then, but as events unfolded, Miss Blazovich and her bad teaching methods convinced my mother that I should go to St. Anthony's Academy for the fifth grade, twenty-seven miles away in Missoula. None of us could have imagined what a fortuitous outcome that would prove to be for our family.

Our mother had made two friends in Arlee: Florence Bouch, the wife of one of the Demer's Mercantile owners, and Cecile Plante, an Indian woman who lived up the track from us. We were all fond of Cecile and her quick, joyous laughter as she helped us around the house and yard. She could do anything. She and my mother had a good time smoking and drinking beer or coffee while they shelled peas or snapped beans for canning. Florence and our mother had much in common, both being artistic and great readers. Florence was tall and regal, cultured, and very Catholic. She, like my mother, had gone to a Catholic college, and when they talked over the situation about Miss Blazovich, came to the conclusion that St. Anthony's parochial day school in Missoula was a good solution for me, and our Catholic benefactor, Ed Lawler, agreed to pay for it. I could stay with Mrs. Sontag, a relative of Florence's, who lived within walking distance of St. Anthony's Academy. Cecile had her own stories of how Indian kids had been treated in the school system and even forced into special schools away from the reservation. In preparation for leaving for St. Anthony's, Cecile, Florence, and my mother conjured up a small but elegant wardrobe for me. In the late afternoon, they would stop for a break and have a glass of beer, and the three of them would laugh and tell stories and then have another beer. They had a good time, and somehow three dresses emerged by the time I was ready to leave.

On a mellow Sunday afternoon in the autumn of 1944, eleven years old, I took the bus from Arlee to Missoula and walked with my one suitcase to Mrs. Sontag's house on 6th Street. The next day, she helped enroll me in the fifth grade, and I attended my first day at St. Anthony's Academy.

Mrs. Sontag was prim and fussy, and believed in young ladies learning manners. So in many respects, living with her was like going to a finishing school. Right away, I was taught how to sit at the table, keep one arm in my lap while I ate, spoon soup without slurping, start the silverware from the outside in, and apply my napkin often. I was to make my bed when I got out of it, put my pajamas away, wash and brush my teeth twice a day.

Life was orderly and routine, with consistent expectations. My mother never visited me there that I remember, though she wrote little notes. It was Budson who dropped in for surprise visits on Saturday and had lunch with us. He made Mrs. Sontag laugh, and she adored him. Once she remarked to him that she was going to make a lady out of me, and he quickly replied, "You cannot make a lady out of my sister, Jo Anne, Mrs. Sontag. She was born that way." She was rebuked, but quickly agreed. I thought he was the cleverest person I had ever met.

I only went into the parlor to practice the piano, or when Mrs. Sontag held her Sunday teas after church with her lady friends, which I was required to attend. They all smelled of talc and lavender, wore little print dresses with hats and gloves, and seemed totally foreign to me in all their finery, their pink nails and faintly blushed cheeks. My mother, with her jeans, white shirt, and cowboy hat belonged to an alien tribe by comparison. They were refined and simple, avoiding anything bold or vulgar, and I assumed ideas were in that same category. I sat there with my beribboned hair, long white stockings and blue dress, carefully balancing a teacup, and longing to be outside roller skating. Time in that parlor stood still like a toothache. When it was finally over, I darted to my room, got my skates, and flew up to the university, because it had a circular sidewalk that surrounded a small forest of trees, and the band might be practicing on the steps of the music school. I didn't know it at the time, of course, but my Salisbury siblings were going to school there. I wonder now if my mother knew that Emma Salisbury lived in Missoula, that close to us, and for the same reason: the university.

After I had been living with Mrs. Sontag about three months, one day my mother showed up and, without much explanation, took me away. She had rented a house in Missoula, and we were all going to live together again. What prompted our mother to leave Arlee and settle in Missoula for the rest of the school year is a mystery, and because change was a constant in our lives, I think we forgot how to ask the why of anything. At the time, it seemed like just one more of our mother's erratic, unmoored decisions. But now, looking back on it, it was provident, too.

We moved several times that fall and winter, because we couldn't pay the rent. The first house was a big airy place with a bathroom and four bedrooms upstairs. I loved that house with its sliding parlor doors and bay window, its air of past glory and gentility. We spent Christmas there, a troubled time with our mother's litany of sorrow for her lost children, Jim and Anneva. For some reason Lennie Cline, out of jail and needing a place to live, came and stayed with us. Our mother was gone for several days, and he cooked the meals and took us for long drives in his car, a small red coupe with a rumble seat. Budson sat in front with Lennie, who was showing him how to drive. Roger and I scrambled into the rumble seat, and somewhere on our journey, Lennie would stop and get us ice cream cones. We loved those outings with Lennie, who was familiar and likeable, like a father. One Saturday morning, the police showed up and arrested him. He had stolen that beautiful little red coupe with the rumble seat. We never saw him again.

Our mother, restless and anxious, was often gone, visiting old friends, seeking their advice, choosing memory over the present to assuage her loneliness. She was a sad, aimless soul wandering the world, seeking moments of reprieve from her dark, unwanted thoughts in the superficial intimacy of bars. Other times, she was sick with a hangover or a migraine headache and was bedridden. Budson was the adult then. He helped us get ready for school before he biked across town to Sentinel High School where he was a junior. Roger and I both attended Sacred Heart Academy, which was close to our neighborhood. St. Anthony's was across town in the more elite, fashionable part of Missoula. My mother was a professed atheist, and the reason we were going to Catholic schools had something to do with our mysterious Catholic benefactor. He was willing to pay for our schooling, plus sending each month the hundred-dollar check for our sustenance, which he did until he died. My mother's opinion of religion was Marxian. It was "an opiate of the people."

Sober, often hungover, our mother would sometimes remember to query us about our schoolwork, our friends, and what we were reading. There was no censorship, and I was reading the *Decameron* by Boccaccio and the *Droll Stories* by Balzac when I was a curious, pubescent eleven-year-old. As we grew older, we were embarrassed and tried to avoid her talks to us about sex.

Budson, protect yourself. You boys know what Trojans are, and what they are for, I presume. You don't want to be looking down the barrel of a loaded shotgun. Jode, don't marry the first boy you go out with. You'll find yourself stuck on a farm out in the middle of nowhere with a passel of snotty-faced kids and a demanding, ignorant mother-in-law.

We turned her advice into humor. When Budson was on his way out the door on a date, we'd remind him, "Got a couple of Trojans in your hip pocket?" Or if a boy showed up looking for me, Budson would mutter, "Passel of snotty-nosed brats in the making, right there."

We often had a "Hansen Family Night" when we all gathered in our mother's bedroom and performed. The evening always began with our pledge, "The Hansens are a funny lot. We'll always stick together, just like this," and we'd cross our fingers. Our mother began the evening with a story of the ranch, but more often, she recited one of her favorite poems, Browning's "My Last Duchess," or Carleton's "Over the Hill to the Poor House, / I'm wending my weary way, / only a woman of seventy, / and just a trifle gray." When she recited this poem, we didn't dare look at each other for fear of bursting out laughing. One time she caught us rolling our eyes and abruptly walked out of the room, insulted, muttering about how heartless we were. When she returned, we quickly apologized. She leveled her sharp eyes on us, and recited an oft-repeated quote from Shakespeare: "*There are more things in heaven and earth, Horatio, than are dreamt of in your philosophy.*" We managed not to laugh. Budson once brought us all to a solemn moment when he recited Marc Antony's speech at the death of Caesar, he was that good. My mother laughed until she cried when he re-cited from *Huckleberry Finn* or *Tom Sawyer.* I usually tap danced or read a poem. But it was Roger, our mother's least favorite, who always ended our programs and held our awed reverence with his soulful renditions of "Red River Valley " or "Shenandoah" on his harmonica. All of our days growing up in Arlee, I remember his whistling, his singing, his hauntingly beautiful harmonica as he played lonesome tunes on long, rainy afternoons. Once, when Roger was playing his harmonica and I dropped my book to listen, Budson painted my portrait. I was a self-conscious girl, embarrassed at how much it looked like me. He titled it, "J listening to R." I'm sorry to say I've lost it in the wanderings of time and place, this artifact of our youth.

46

Budson began telling our mother tales of this friend he had made at Sentinel High in Missoula. According to his stories, this boy argued with teachers, contradicted their facts, and was often suspended. He was, Budson avowed, a genius, and had at his fingertips more information than the *Encyclopedia Britannica*. My mother began encouraging Budson to bring the "genius" home. She wanted to meet him. One evening that winter, reading in my room, I heard voices in the kitchen. Some time later, I heard a familiar "thump" and guessed my mother had fainted, as was her theatrical habit on hearing good, bad, or even indifferent news. There was a scramble of excitement, nothing unusual as far as our lives were concerned, and then my mother was at my bedroom door with a tall, lanky boy. *This is your brother Stanley*, she announced. What I saw was a boy with blue-black hair combed straight back, glasses as thick as a beer bottle, and wearing a long dark overcoat with a white silk scarf. He held a cigarette between nicotine-stained fingers.

Our mother, on meeting him, had asked about his parents, and found out that they were from Plentywood. His mother was Alice Young, the young librarian with whom my father had had a brief affair before he met my mother. My mother remembered what Rodney had revealed to her those many years ago about a boy he had fathered, and seventeen years later, that very boy, thinking he was an only child, discovered he had nine siblings. His best friend, Budson, was also his brother.

That spring when school was out, our mother was anxious to move back to our farm at Arlee. The familiar seed catalogs from the nursery in Helena had arrived in the mail, and she was excited about planting the garden. Despite my protests because our house was so small, Stanley came with us. I recall his mother and my mother standing in the yard at Arlee and briefly talking. By some quirk of fate, Alice Young Iverson had been a teacher at Arlee High School the same year I went to school at St. Anthony's, and was Budson's English teacher until they joined me in Missoula. I don't know if my mother knew any of this or not. When they met at our place, they both knew who the other was, according to my mother, but never acknowledged it. When Alice left that day, it was understood that Stanley was staying with us.

Years later, I asked Stanley what his mother had said when he told her about his newly discovered father and family. Stanley replied that he never told his mother that he knew her secret. It wasn't until she died that he told his daughter, Shana, that I was her aunt. I found this news amazing, but reflecting on it later, understood this was just another reason why I was so fond of this brother.

When Stanley Iverson enrolled in Arlee High School, he caused the same disruptions that he had at Missoula Sentinal, only worse. His erudition was unmatched by the teachers, and they could only express outrage and hostility that he dared to challenge their knowledge. He seldom attended school, preferring to stay home and read books. On the days my mother prevailed upon him to go to school, we would start out, but he was miserable and would talk me out of going, too, and we would return home to read books, or I would make up a play where he was always the butler, Jeeves, and did my bidding. My mother would express her outrage and insist we go to school, especially me. *Stanley, for god's sake, your sister needs to go to school. If you don't want to go, then don't, but don't talk her into being delinquent with you. Jesus H. Christ!* He only frowned at her, pursed his lips, and stubborn but dignified, ignored her. She couldn't stare him down. He appeased her sometimes by telling her he would be my tutor, but that only meant reading and talking about books. Toward spring, we went to school more, and Stanley would meet me in my classroom, where I was always making up work. He met my teacher, Miss O'Hara, and they would have long conversations. Sometimes, he would leave at night, and Budson said he was meeting his new girlfriend, Miss O'Hara. That really upset my mother. *Stanley, if the school board gets even a whiff of this knowledge, her job will be on the line. She is a good teacher, and the students like her, and she's helping Jo Anne catch up. Think about how you are compromising her!* Frowning, he didn't say a thing, didn't even look up from his book.

Stanley had strange habits, which all three of us mocked and teased him about, as siblings do. He hated bathing with a passion, and my mother had to cajole him to get his long legs into the Saturday night tub in the kitchen. He would never peel or eat an orange because it made his hands sticky. He liked grilled cheese sandwiches, and he would eat them with endless cups of black coffee. I can see him now, sitting at the kitchen table in his overcoat with the white scarf, even on the warmest days, reading Swinburne aloud, or other romantic poets whom he loved. Sometimes he would get up and with great, wide flourishes read Poe, or Byron, or Keats aloud. This always made me laugh, and sometimes my mother would come in from the garden and watch and laugh, too. She liked him and often said he was more like our father than any of us in his mannerisms and political savvy. I often went to sleep, hearing the murmur of their voices in the kitchen as they drank beer and she told him stories about his father. Once, I heard her say, *Do you think of Jo Anne as your soul sister?* I couldn't hear his muffled reply, but I was perplexed by the question, the word "soul." What did it mean?

He stayed with us for two years, then our mother surprised us one day by sending him home to his family in Spokane, declaring, *He undermines my authority.* Budson was in the Navy by then, and Roger and I walked with our sad brother to the train station and waved him away.

47

About a year after Stanley left, one day in late autumn of 1947, when I returned from school, my mother was crying, writing a letter. She was sober, concentrating. *This afternoon, Mr. Ryan, the station master, delivered a telegram from my brother Colie, saying that Papa is sick. I'm writing my folks, asking if I can come home. I want to see Papa before he dies.* It seemed strange to me that she had to ask permission to see her parent, and I mentioned it. "Why do you have to ask to come home? Can't you just go and see your parents? I wouldn't have to write you, would I, if I lived far away, and ask if I could come home?"

Time passes, Jode, and weeks turn into months, months into years. They have never been interested in my children, especially Mama. Now, I'd like to go home and see them all. Aside from Colie and Eva, I haven't seen my parents or brothers and sisters for twenty-five years. Maybe, after so many years, I can visit. It's worth a try.

I mailed that letter, and then there was the long wait for an answer. Sitting around the table studying, we'd pass notes. "Any news from the relatives we don't know?" Roger wrote.

Our mother stayed sober, waiting.

One afternoon when we returned from school, she was packing a suitcase, elated. Her father had written, telling her to come home. *He called me Mariesie, said he missed me, wanted me to come. He said they both wanted me to come, even Mama!*

It was a different mother we watched become a daughter and sister to kin in a different land. She was aglow with happiness. We were outsiders looking in, curious, but feeling remote from it all, the way we felt remote from those other siblings in Wolf Point.

I don't remember how it all came about, but I went with my mother to the West Coast to see her parents and her family. We took the bus, and I recall a long, cold trip through small Montana and Idaho towns with bitter winds and snowstorms. When we arrived in Seaside, my first glimpse of the ocean was the incoming tide rushing down the streets of the small resort town.

I was fourteen years old when I met my grandmother. My grandfather Chapman died before we arrived. My mother was heartbroken, full of regret that she had not seen him before he died. She mourned him the rest of her life.

One thing I saw that the Chapman siblings had in common was that at any gathering, there was an excuse to drink. Whiskey was their drink of choice, though beer was always on hand, too. Nervous and anxious, my mother joined them. Downing shot after shot, they talked about their missing father, and reminisced about life on the Montana ranch. The more they drank, the more emotional and volatile they became. They brought up old grievances, and arguments would break out over some perceived injury. People with hurt feelings would get up and stalk out, then come back, usually with a new supply of booze. A few more drinks, and they were maudlin, apologizing, making amends, laughing. Despite the tumultuous times they created when they were together drinking, I felt kinship with them. They were quick to laughter, affectionate, and curious about each other's children.

Colie was the first to quit drinking, and talked to Billy (Eva) about getting sober. It took years, but eventually all the Chapmans, using family intervention, helped each other quit drinking and stay sober.

I did not get to know my grandmother, who was polite and formal. She was remote with me and my mother, treating us much differently than the other family members. It was easy to see that my mother was uncomfortable around her. They didn't have much to say to one another, and after one week, we left.

Through the years, if any of the Chapman relatives were in the area, they would stop and see me. I remember especially a visit from my mother's sister, Aunt Ann, and her husband, Art. They were on their way to Chicago for a daughter's wedding. Ann was ecstatic to be back in Montana, and was consumed with nostalgia about the Plentywood ranch. When I suggested coffee, she wanted to know if I had whiskey, and I immediately went to the liquor store and got a bottle of Jim Beam, which they ruined.

Around Christmastime, for many years, I would get a box of walnuts and filberts from their farm in Oregon.

By some quirk of fate, it was my brother Jim who became a part of the Chapman family on the West Coast. When he graduated from the university in Missoula, he got jobs teaching music in Seaside, Warrenton, and, finally, Astoria, Oregon, where he lived until he died. Though he never had much of a mother growing up, as an adult, all of her Chapman relatives were his family.

48

My mother's ten years of drinking, debt, poverty, and worry took its toll on all of us. Grown, we escaped, absorbed in our own lives. After our benefactor, Ed Lawler, died, she was desperate, still drinking, and riddled with anxiety. Creditors were at the door, demanding payment. I once saw her cavalierly toss some bills in the stove saying, *My god, they must think I'm made of money. I have nothing to feed these hungry wolves!* There was one bill with the bold letters of the Missoula Mercantile. It was the store where she bought the best linens to embroider, the pillow tubing she had hemstitched and then embroidered, the elegant linen especially sized and stamped for dresser scarves. There was the regular bill, always ignored, from the Book of the Month club. Roger and I were incredulous.

During that time, she put an ad in North and South Dakota papers in the "Wanted" section: "Widow, owns ten acre farm, looking for a business partner." At various times, a man would show up and then leave a few days later. One, Grover Anderson, she had a lengthy correspondence with. He often included a five- or ten-dollar bill in his letters. He was excited about the partnership, believing it would happen, but it never did.

There was one man, though, she liked, and it was by sheer chance that I met him. It was when I was going to high school in Missoula my sophomore year, living with friends. Crossing Higgins Bridge, I recognized my mother wearing a new dress and high heels, holding hands with this tall, attractive older man. When she saw me, she dropped his hand and quickly introduced me. His name was Arthur Cameron, and he was from North Dakota. He was friendly, affable. A few days later, I got a note from her saying she and Arthur had many interests in common. He was a Socialist, a union man, of Scottish heritage, and he was going to stick around. She mentioned that Roger liked him, and they fished together. She sounded happy. Busy with my own life, I forgot about them. Much later, I heard from Roger that she returned from town one day and he was gone, no note or anything. She never heard from Arthur again.

Many years later, she mentioned Arthur briefly. *He was a nice lover . . . I guess he thought I was a rich widow.* And she gave me that little knowing, ironic smile.

The men kept coming. Roger and I often challenged her about this, resenting her duplicity with these strangers who invaded our lives with an assumed authority. She was mostly vague and noncommittal, but I remember one stark message from her. *Don't you know, Jode, that if they could, they would take advantage of me? Don't waste your sympathy on them. Opportunistic scoundrels, all of them.*

49

It's commonly thought that we only tend to remember the good things, and the bad things are locked in a mental closet to save us from the pain of recall. When I remember the dark events, they seem like necessary rebukes that surge through the veil to remind me of needed lessons, or so I like to believe. One such memory has its own psychic reasons for being. Perhaps, better phrased, it is a haunting moment of shame that I regret. It happened in the most unpremeditated way possible, which astonishes me when I recall it. I can see it all in exact detail, as if time slowed it up for my attention.

Budson and Jim surprise us by coming home for the weekend from college. Roger is a junior, I am a senior in high school. We have gathered around the kitchen table drinking coffee, smoking cigarettes, in a moment of good humor and camaraderie. We are being funny and witty in easy and familiar ways, and there is much hilarity and laughter in appreciation for who we are. We like being together. I am reading Hardy's *Jude the Obscure* (Budson makes us laugh by referring to me as "Jude the Obscene"), and Budson and Jim have just read and been impressed with Conrad's *Heart of Darkness*. Ideas circle the table, and our mother comes in, curious. She says something about Conrad, and we pause, then go on with our own conversation. She tries to enter the discussion again, and once again we hesitate, and then go on as if she hasn't spoken. As I write this, I can see her face crumbling with hurt, her anguished realization that we don't need her anymore, that we are way beyond that. *You won't let me in, not one of you,* she cries. She goes to her bedroom and closes the door. We turn quiet and can hear her muffled sobs floating into the kitchen, into our hearts. We are silent, not looking at each other, ashamed.

Without a word, we had conspired against her. Our common history united us, and was the demise of her power. We had grown up and over her. Anneva, married and living still in Wolf Point, made her a grandmother. That spring I was graduating from high school, Budson was getting married, and Roger was joining the Navy. The autumn of 1952, Budson, Jim, and I were all students at the University of Montana. Budson, as well as being a painter and an actor, majored in English literature, and I did as well. Jim was a trumpet player with the Moon Moods, a popular band, and a music major. Our mother was proud. She revered artists and teachers above all. *They will save us*, she often said, *with their courage of imagination.*

None of us, reflecting about the past, could remember when our mother quit drinking for good, got a job, and even joined Alcoholics Anonymous. We figured it was about the same time our father's friend in Butte died, and the hundred dollars he sent each month suddenly stopped. When the incident above took place, she had been sober a month, but it took us a long time to believe this was a serious attempt to really quit, since we had been down that path many times before. *John Barleycorn is a tempting bedfellow*, she would later reflect. *By the time I jilted him for sobriety, and looked at my life, it gradually dawned on me that in the ten or more years of drink, life had passed me by. I had missed out on those important changes in my children's lives, and then you were gone, really gone. You were strangers I had cultivated through years of drinking. That, Jode, was the hardest part of getting and staying sober. I had to face the most difficult person in the world, myself.*

She was, to my knowledge, never drunk again. The core of her, the lonely woman whose temperament had made her an outsider, was always present, though. Drinking had only been a temporary reprieve. She was always conscious that she was outside of conventionality because of her radical beliefs and her choices in life. She was rather shy and had few friends. After the death of Florence Bouch, Cecile Plante was her one lasting friend and confidante, a constant, loyal presence. So few women she knew were even remotely interested in her politics, her ideas, her experiences.

Sober, she confronted the world alone, always a radical, and shaped a new life. She got a job as a nurse's aid in St. Patrick's Hospital in Missoula and joined a carpool to get to work. She began to turn her dreams into reality, an amazing transformation to witness. Sam, a friend from her old bar days, mostly sober, showed up to put an addition on the house in exchange for room, board and pocket money. They found out that they had both voted for Norman Thomas in 1944 and 1948 when he ran for president on the Socialist ticket for the last time. To my mother, these were great credentials. Thomas, the "Clergyman Socialist," had run for president six times, beginning in 1928. He was an old familiar to the liberals of the time, and my mother belonged to the ACLU, which he founded, and had been his presidential elector from Montana. Between bouts of sobriety, and long political discussions, Sam finally completed the new edition on the old farmhouse at Arlee.

No longer drinking, she saved her money and, with Cecile's help, planted trees, flowers, and a voluptuous garden. She continued to take prizes for her flower arrangements at the county fair. Her needlework and crocheting were artistic and unusual, as was her needlepoint. Generous by nature, she would send visitors off with their arms laden with her garden bounty; her meticulous and artistic embroidery on the finest linen were welcomed gifts.

She tried to get together with us, but we were busy with new friends, our studies, our interesting lives. I had a part-time job as a bookkeeper at a cleaners on Main Street, and she used to wander by, a lonesome figure, showing me she was sad and missing me. There was that little prickle of guilt, a touch of impatience as I waved at her and ducked my head back into my work. I was in love and could think of little else. The times I had lunch with her, it was all about McCarthyism, the Korean War, and the controversial Kinsey report titled *Sexual Behavior of the Human Female.*

Imagine our Democracy and Bill of rights being submitted to the meanest spirit of totalitarianism! McCarthy with his accusations and fear mongering will destroy this country. He and his cronies are ignorant, shameless, and their tactics emulate the foe they despise!

Or worse: *It's about time someone explored women's sexuality, instead of assuming purity exchanged for motherhood was every chaste woman's goal.*

I would make an exit as fast as I could.

That spring of my freshman year and just as Budson was getting ready to graduate, we got subpoenaed to go to court. Our mother was being sued for money she had received from Grover Anderson for a partnership in the farm. It was an embarrassing trial, with Budson and me called to the witness stand, ignorant of the details, unable to answer questions.

We knew about Anderson, but we didn't know about the $3,000 he had given her for a partnership in the farm. What we saw was a rather feeble, inarticulate, angry old man, trying to get justice after being wronged by our mother. The jury returned with a guilty verdict, and the judge ordered her to give Anderson restitution. It never happened, though. He died, a broken and bitter man, not too long after the trial.

On the way back to Missoula, Budson was grim, and we spoke little. We didn't have to. He had been married that previous spring to a respectable, affluent girl, and his wife was pregnant. We were students at the university, surrounded by people from well-cultivated, respectable families. We felt the separation, the difference in our status keenly. We knew, from an early age, that we would have to forge our destinies out of this difference, this alienation. This trial was just another reminder.

Budson dropped me off at the dorm, and I was almost at the door when he called me back. "When she dies," he said, "I don't want to know about it."

I saw Budson, now called Howard, only one more time at the university. I had an errand at Main Hall, the oldest, most elegant building on campus. This was where we paid our fees, changed classes, applied for scholarships, sought information. I was running up the steps, and I passed him as he was running down. I glanced back, and saw him briefly pause, and then go on. Like strangers, we never spoke. We had outgrown our mother's plea not to be separated.

Roger came to see me once, but didn't stay long. "I don't belong here with you and Budson and this school. I've got to head back, catch the bus . . . I just wanted you both to know I'm joining the Navy."

I still have the mental image of his retreating figure, tall, skinny, head down, striding off.

Through the years, Stanley and I were always in touch. Intelligent as he was, he never went to college. Instead, he became an anarchist, a Communist, and an activist, well-known and admired in Seattle. Articulate and well-read, he organized two bookstores, one called The Id and the other, Red and Black Books. He was a steady presence at the Blue Moon saloon, where he held court of an evening with area intellectuals, many of them professors at the University of Washington. Painters found him an interesting study, this lanky, long-haired bearded man with a leather cap and jacket, boots, and hippy grace. His portrait is an interesting presence in establishments in Seattle. With several other people, he started a cooperative pizza business in an old garage, and the workers shared the profits according to need and the hours they worked. He was the perfect example of the alternative lifestyle exemplified by the 1970s: not married, living with his special friend, Barbara, and their daughter, Shana, in a houseboat on Lake Union.

It was inevitable that he would meet the Emma Salisbury family who had moved from Missoula to Seattle in the late 1940s. His life seemed fraught with significant meetings. At a rally against the Vietnam War, he met a young woman he was attracted to, and they spent time together. As they were becoming acquainted, revealing facts about their pasts, they realized that she was his niece, Colleen Salisbury, the daughter of Rodney's oldest son, Mike. It was a fortuitous meeting, and through Colleen, he met them all—Emma, Mike, Gene, Jardis, and Camilla (Pat Salisbury was killed during World War II)—and they recognized him without question as their kin, their father's son in both looks and political fervor. Emma, who knew nothing of this son before he arrived at her doorstep with her granddaughter, Colleen, assumed that this was proof that though Rodney's attention wandered, she, Emma, was the important one, the wife. My mother was just another one of his distractions, albeit one lasting thirteen years.

It was during one of my visits with Stanley that he mentioned that Emma wanted to meet me. My mother was alive at the time, and I found the idea ludicrous. "Tell her 'no,' Stanley. It will never happen. Tell her also I'm claiming the name she wouldn't give to me legally—I am, as of this moment, Jo Anne Salisbury Troxel."

My mother, an old woman then, had suffered too many losses in her life. One of the most painful was the loss of her son, Budson, an estrangement none of us ever quite understood. I knew she didn't approve of Barbara, the woman he married, considering her bourgeoisie and middle class with her safe and ordinary life. Had Barbara been an artist, or a teacher, or quirky and weird, even neurotic in some way, she would have won my mother's approval. Just being a healthy, normal-functioning human being got her no kudos from our mother. When Budson, or Howard as he was now referred to, called that spring to ask me to get some of our family together for his wedding, our mother refused to go, as did my brother Jim, who found Barbara dull, ordinary, and a Republican. Anneva, her husband, Ed, Roger, and I traveled to Billings to represent Howard's family and attend his June wedding in 1952, a few days after I graduated from high school. It was hard to visualize my mother comfortable in such a home where the wedding took place. She would have snobbishly scorned the wealth of it, and the lack of originality.

It was about nine months later, after his first daughter, Carolyn, was born, that the rift occurred and lasted.

Howard, living in Billings and working for his father-in-law, was a happy and proud father, and in the flush of this happiness, relented, and invited our mother to come to Billings and meet her granddaughter. It wasn't until years later that I found out what happened one evening when Howard was working late, and our mother and Barbara were alone. They bandied words, and incensed over something, our mother dramatically stormed out of the house into the dark night. What I knew was that when I would ask about Howard, our mother was evasive, saying she hadn't heard from him. Now, I think she was waiting for him to make the first move, but he never did. He was twenty-five years old when Carolyn was born, and he and our mother never saw each other or spoke again.

I think I understood at the time the overwhelming responsibility she had put upon him taking care of his two younger siblings, her years of absence, neglect, and drinking. It totaled up as the days of his youth. There were times of tension, and I remember late night arguments between them when he returned from the Navy and learned that she had carelessly spent the allotment checks the Navy sent home each month. She had promised to save the money for him when he was discharged. And the subpoena that had forced us to court was just another one of the many incidents that added to his long list of disappointments and embarrassments. Whatever Barbara told Howard about their argument, he took his wife's side, and summarily dismissed his mother from his children's lives. Years later, I found out from Howard that during their quarrel, Barbara had said in anger to my mother, "How do you think my father felt that I had married into such white trash?" I understood, finally, that from such a remark, there was no going back.

For years, Howard didn't contact me, either, since I was associated with our mother. Before she died, I asked her once if she regretted losing him, if she missed him.

I wouldn't recognize him if I met him on the street now, Jode, he would be forty-five years old. It's gone. He is a successful businessman, owns an airplane, has a lovely family. He's naturally artistic, and I hope he still paints. There wasn't a place for me in this new life of his, you and I and Jim know that. He's a Republican, another way he can deny the old life, the old values of his upbringing. I'm glad, though, he still sees Roger, that he's kept that one connection in his life. Roger is welcome to his home with their family. But not you, not Jim, certainly not Stanley. We both laughed at that, knowing how Stanley abjured bathing and always smelled a little musty, like he lived in a basement.

Over the years, busy with my life, my family, my teaching career in Bozeman, I would occasionally see Howard on one of his business trips. He would be cordial, but brief. There was no thought of our getting together, though I lived in Bozeman and he lived in Billings, a couple of hours away. I was not an aunt to his three daughters, nor did I even know them until they were grown. I always felt sad and missed him for the rest of the day after one of those chance encounters, but I also accepted it. I never mentioned it to my mother. Why bring it up and make her unhappy?

Restless and lonely, our mother advertised in Oregon and California papers that she had experience taking care of old and disabled people, and had good references. She was always able to get a job, and at first she would welcome the adventure and was able to make herself indispensable to the people she helped. But come spring, she always wanted to be back in Montana, planting a garden, tending to trees and flowers at Arlee with Cecile, and she would return. The last and best job she ever had was with Judge Bescanson, retired, a widower. She could work for him and also tend to her garden and flowers in Arlee. He had a lovely old house on Eddy Avenue in Missoula, and he hired our mother to take care of the house and oversee the many social events he hosted at his home. There was also a cook and a housekeeper, and she was to instruct them as to their duties. It was the perfect job for her. She would call me, excited, about a dinner she had planned and how pleased the judge was, as well as the guests. I think this was the happiest time in my mother's life. When I visited her, she prepared tea for us. It was a lovely moment, my mother pouring at the head of the table, passing around her lovely croissants and cream puffs on china plates, the judge praising her, their easy bantering. "Now Marie, promise me that there will be cream puffs and a spot of tea, and I'll join the revolution with you," he teased. My husband, Vern, loved to comment, "She's the perfect bourgeoisie revolutionary, isn't she."

At ninety-three, the judge died in his sleep, and my mother helped his two sons close up the house and put it up for sale. It was a disappointing and sad time for her, and she never recovered from the loss. I measure her physical decline from that time. Never had she been more lonesome than after the judge died, at least not since she'd lost Rodney.

51

She was a hypochondriac, always fearing an early death, and then one day there were the facts: She had lung blockage, osteoporosis, and hardening of the arteries. She was advised to live at sea level, and since Roger lived in California, she left her beloved Arlee home and went to be with him.

Roger had a medical discharge from the Navy after a psychotic break, and because of his erratic behavior, had been clinically labeled schizophrenic. He had always been physically frail, weighing a mere 130 pounds for his six-foot frame. Alcohol and drugs exacerbated his unruly temperament, and several times he had been in mental institutions, one time because he was walking down a city street in the wee hours of the morning naked except for his shoes, singing and talking to himself. Everyone who knew him agreed he was brilliant, wonderfully handsome, witty, and charming. It wasn't unusual for his psychiatrist, at any particular time, to also be his friend and buddy. This used to make him laugh. The drugs they prescribed kept him as balanced as he could ever be. Then during a physical examination, it was discovered he needed an operation for a hernia. He awoke from the operation in Loma Linda Hospital with a battery of doctors surrounding his bed. They had discovered he had a tumor, "carcinoid syndrome," and six weeks later, they operated, taking out so much of his bowel that he was left with what they called a "short gut." They gave him drugs to slow down his digestion so he could absorb nutrients from his food. He was razor-blade thin and looked older than his years, except for his hair. It was auburn, wavy with little tendrils framing his gaunt face. Our mother knew all about his troubles, and felt that she could help him, and he was pleased to have her come and live with him. It was a strange and fitful alliance between two people who had little in common and had never gotten along well. As adults, they had their baggage, hers of being a remorseful mother, and his of lasting anger and resentment because of her treatment of him as a boy. As adults, they fared little better, though they tried. The formula was wrong. He wanted to be a son she could love, and she wanted to be a worthy mother. It was a disaster from the beginning. They had terrible quarrels that further tore them apart. At the same time, her health was deteriorating day by day. Eventually, she had to go to a nursing home, and then to assisted living. The osteoporosis in her spine was causing constant pain, she had difficulty breathing, and her heart was failing. I let my sister Anneva know she was ill and suggested we fly out to see her, a surprise visit from her two daughters. But Anneva declined, saying she was busy and not feeling well herself. A mother is a powerful person in a child's life, something I learned from my sister Anneva. She had missed out on all the drunken, chaotic times, the turmoil and uncertainty of our lives; at the same time, she never discovered the intellectual rewards of reading, the emphasis on art and culture, the love of words that belonged to us. She not only lost her mother, but she was a stranger to all of her siblings, her full brother, Jim, included. She was always at the window, seeing all the vitality on the other side, but never able to join it. It made her resentful, angry, and sad.

I called my mother every Saturday morning, and we talked about her health, books, education, and politics, always politics. *There's a revolution going on, Jode, and it's the young people. They know this system is rigged against them, and they want no part of this horrible capitalistic war in Vietnam. Does anyone in the world know why we are there except those profiteers of death, the munitions makers? People are taking to the streets! I'm missing your father, Pet. He would be out marching with these young people, cheering them on!* She was pleased when I told her I was one of the marchers. *Your father's daughter,* she said.

Toward the end, I asked her about dying, if she were afraid. I remembered that she had once dabbled in Rosicrucianism.

I'm not afraid of dying at all. I'm in constant pain now. I never thought I would be a dependent old woman, but that's what I am. How did I get so old so soon, Jode? What happened to my days of wine and roses? Who is that old woman in the mirror? Where did it all go?

I asked her about the afterlife, this hardened atheist, and was saddened by her answer: *There has to be more to it than this life, Jode. It has not been enough for me, when I consider it all.*

When I hung up the phone, I cried.

52

The summer of 1975, my husband, Vern, and our seven-year-old daughter, Allison, and I traveled to California to see her. She took us for lunch, as was her habit, and I can still see her worn freckled hand holding her wallet, and remember thinking how generous she always was. While we were waiting to be served, we had a few moments alone. *I won't be here when you return next year, Jode,* she said matter of factly. *I want to thank you for buying the Arlee place, keeping it in the family. I'd like my granddaughter Allison to have it some day. There's the burial insurance, as you know, and it should take care of my cremation.*

I said the usual things, that she was having a bad day, that we would be back, as usual, next summer, that if she needed me, I would come.

After lunch, we took her back to the rest home, a lovely place with a wide expanse of green lawn, a welcoming living room. Old women with groomed hair and make-up sat at tables playing bridge, talking and laughing. We said goodbye to her there, and she bent down and hugged Allison, saying, *Don't forget me, your grandmother, who loves you very much.*

I was walking out the door and glanced back at her, the lonely little figure, head down, looking lost and forlorn like an abandoned child. I ran back, and as I hugged her, I was the child, losing my mother, and weeping at the loss. She let me cry, and all she said was, *I want to die in Arlee, Jode. Not here in this phony place with these old sizzerbill ladies.*

That was the last time I saw her.

Before we left town, I called Roger, and asked him to see her or call every day, as she was frail, and feeling mortal. He promised.

I was at school the day the call came. It was Vern, telling me the rest home in San Bernardino had called, and that R. Marie Chapman Hansen had died several days before, but they had been unable to reach their contact, Roger Hansen. Finally, one of the nurses remembered a daughter in Bozeman and had my information. That was how we found out. Her birthday was January the first, and she was seventeen days into her seventy-fifth year when she died. I grieved that she had died alone, our mother who had been so alone in life. I got this notion that in the end, in her final moments as she slipped from this mortal world, she told herself a story and imagined she was back in Plentywood roaming the prairie, searching for treasures with her dog, Fen. That image carried my grief to a safe place.

I went to California to be with Roger and help him with the final details of her life in the rest home. I found him in a bar, drinking beer, playing his guitar and singing.

"You weren't there," I said. "You promised."

"You don't know what it was like. No matter what I did, I couldn't please her. Everything for her was that goddamn revolution, the ugly capitalists, the bourgeoisie. I was sick of it!"

He was crying, wiping the tears furiously from his face. He was the frustrated, angry little boy I remembered. We sat quietly, feeling the strange emptiness of our world without her.

"When she went to AA meetings, she always fouled it up by saying, 'I am R. Marie Hansen, a revolutionary, union organizer, a Socialist, and an alcoholic.' She never missed a lick. Jeez!"

We gave each other a long look, then laughed helplessly.

"She was complicated and difficult," he said soberly. "But she loved my son, Keith, and your Allison. At eight years old, how much will they remember?"

"We'll tell them all the stories about the ranch, the revolution. It will be their inheritance, their legacy. Montana will be their mythical home."

At the rest home, the people were nice, fascinated that I was from Montana. "Is there really all that open space, miles and miles without a house in sight?"

"Believe every story she told you," I said.

"She sure loved all those cowboy shows on TV: *Have Gun Will Travel*, *Wagon Train*, *Gunsmoke*. Never missed one. Loved those horses and cowboys, all that open country."

"She grew up on a ranch," I said. Checking out at the desk, I was told she had left a small sum of money, and legally, before I could pass it on to Roger, I had to have all of her children sign off on it.

That was how my brother, Howard, came to know of the death of his mother, and came back to us.

On the plane back to Montana I felt disembodied, living in an unfamiliar space of loss and regret. Maybe that was why, for a brief spell, I had the overwhelming sense that my mother had subsumed my body as her own. My physical stance, leaning forward, was her posture. For those brief moments in the darkness of the plane, I was my mother, going back to her beloved Montana.

Startled, I woke up with the plane roaring onto the tarmac of the Bozeman airport.

Two years later, Roger, drunk, died in a car accident. I was grateful that I did not have to tell her the details. His Fiat with the gas tank in the back was struck and went up in flames.

It couldn't be a nicer day in Seattle, or more fraught with meaning. I am on my way to Lake Union and the *Ora Elwell*, the boat where Stanley lives. As I approach, I see he is on the deck, painting.

"You look like you've been sticking pigs," I say, looking at his red-splattered feet in thongs.

"Just got her back from being repaired. Sprung a leak."

"I told you one more book and she'd go under."

"Did you talk to Jardis? The number I gave you, was it the right one?"

"Yes, we've talked. Next time I'm in town, the three of us are having lunch at the Bon."

He nods, and I can tell he is pleased. I hug him, he smells familiar, musty. "Thanks for being the go-between. I'm excited to meet my sisters."

As I'm leaving, I look back at him and yell, "Vive the Revolution!"

He waves, gives me the peace sign, and smiles that wide Salisbury smile.

Prairie Born
(For my mother, 1/1/01 – 1/17/76)

The last time I saw you,
you were a Montana transplant
stubbornly refusing to take root in California.

The bold bougainvillea,
trees of roses,
fragrant orange blossoms,
lush abundance
affronted you,
Montana and prairie born.

Impatient with the fecundity,
monotony of spilled passion,
that dulled your senses into
withdrawal, boredom,
you hued through the thicket
the underbrush,
with your sharp whetted memory
to the time and place of your beginnings:
the clean prairie,
the sharp smell of sage,
two notes of the Mourning Dove,
the dry bleached bones,
those friendly and familiar deaths.

Here in this place,
in this time
this misnomered rest home
in a fecund world,
you moved your dry bones among
these hot-house plants,
these painted faces,
these plumed exotic birds.

One day you slumbered through
A breakfast, a lunch, a dinner.
frail synapsis finally snapping,
you dreamed of dried bones under pale prairie skies
to be startled awake by California matrons
shocked and affronted by your
ready, willing, and waiting mortality.

Jo Anne Salisbury Troxel
(January 1, 1990)

WHO IS WHO IN THE
SALISBURY HANSEN FAMILIES

Rodney Salisbury was the father of ten children by three different mothers: Emma Ryan Salisbury, Alice Young Iverson, and Marie Chapman Hansen.

Emma and Rodney were married from 1912 to 1938, when Rodney died of a cerebral hemorrhage. They had six children together.

Alice and Rodney had a brief affair, which resulted in one child, Stanley Iverson. Alice married Orville Iverson shortly after she became pregnant with Stanley, Rodney's son.

Marie and Rodney had a loving relationship for thirteen years, from around 1925 until Rodney's death in 1938, and together they had three children.

Marie married Peter Andrew Hansen in 1922, and they were the parents of two children, James Albert and Anneva Grace. Marie was able to obtain a divorce from Peter Andrew Hansen eventually, but Emma refused to give Rodney a divorce that would allow Marie and Rodney to marry legally.

Rodney Salisbury (1887-1938) married Emma Ryan (1885-1979)
in 1912.
Children:
    Michael: 1914-1985
    Janis: 1918-1932 (twin of Jardis)
    Jardis: 1918-1998
    Eugene: 1919-1981
    Camilla: 1921-2004
    Patrick: 1925-1944

Rodney Salisbury and Alice Young Iverson (1902-1983)
Child:
    Stanley Iverson: 1927-1985

Marie Chapman Hansen and Peter Andrew Hansen (1891-1979),
    married in 1922.
    Children:
        James Albert: 1924-2018
        Anneva Grace: 1926-2009

Rodney Salisbury and Marie Chapman Hansen (1901-1976)
    Children:
        Howard Froberg: 1928-2002
        Jo Anne Adaire: 1933-
        Kay Roger: 1935-1978

ENDNOTES

1   Verlaine Stoner McDonald, *The Red Corner*. (Helena, Montana Historical Society Press, 2010), p. 48.

2   McDonald, *The Red Corner*, p. 56.

3   Nick Salvatore, *Eugene V. Debs: Citizen and Socialist*, 2nd ed. (University of Illinois Press, Chicago & Urbana, 1982, 2010), p. 295.

4   James Chace, *1912: Wilson, Roosevelt, Taft and Debs*. (Simon and Schuster Paperbacks, Rockefeller Center, 1230 Avenue of the Americas, New York, NY, 2005), p. 86.

5   Ibid., p. 87.

6   Webb: Chroniclingamerica.loc gov, Historic American Newspapers, *The Producers News* (1918, 1937), U.S. Newspaper Directory.

7   At the end of the CD movie *Reds,* Beatty is interviewed and he mentions this. I also found it on the internet under *Reds*, the movie directed by Warren Beatty.

8   Gerald Zahavi, "Who's Going to Dance with Somebody Who Calls You a Mainstreeter: Communism, Culture, and Community in Sheridan County, Montana, 1918–1934." *Great Plains Quarterly*, University of Nebraska, Lincoln, 1995.) pp. 268–270.

9   Ibid., p. 272

10   McDonald, *The Red Corner*, p. 158.

11   Ibid., p. 159.

12   Ibid., p. 272.

13   Zahavi, "Who's Going to Dance with Somebody Who Calls You a Mainstreeter?", p. 251.

14   McDonald, *The Red Corner*, p. 160.

15   Zahavi, "Who's Going to Dance with Somebody Who Calls You a Mainstreeter?", p. 277.

16   William C. Pratt, "Rural Radicalism on the Northern Plains," (Helena, *Montana: The Magazine of Western History*, Winter, 1992). p. 48.

17   McDonald, *The Red Corner*, p. 171.

18   Ibid.

19   Zahavi, "Who's Going to Dance with Somebody Who Calls You a Mainstreeter?," p. 278.

20   Ibid., p. 280.

21   McDonald, *The Red Corner*, p. 177.

22   Internet: "Trotsky in Mexico. History Today: Trotsky Offered Asylum in Mexico." After he was formally condemned to death in Moscow, the Mexican government offered Trotsky refuge and protection on December 6, 1936.

23   Penelope Lively, *Dancing Fish and Ammonites: A Memoir* (Penguin Group, 375 Hudson Street, New York, NY 2015), p. 116.

BIBLIOGRAPHY

Books:

Chace, James, *1912: Wilson, Roosevelt, Taft and Debs: The Election that Changed the Country,* Simon and Schuster Paperbacks, Rockefeller Center, 1230 Avenue of the Americas, New York, NY, 2005.

Lively, Penelope, *Dancing Fish and Ammonites: A Memoir,* Penguin Group, 375 Hudson Street, New York, NY, 2015.

McDonald, Verlaine Stoner, *The Red Corner: The Rise and Fall of Communism in Northeastern Montana,* Helena, Montana Historical Society Press, 2010.

Salvatore, Nick, *Eugene V. Debs: Citizen and Socialist,* second edition, University of Illinois Press, Urbana & Chicago, 1982, 2007.

Magazines:

Pratt, William C. "Rural Radicalism on the Northern Plains, 1912–1950." *Montana: The Magazine of Western History,* Winter, 1992.

Zahavi, Gerald: "Who's Going to Dance with Somebody Who Calls You a Mainstreeter: Communism, Culture, and Community in Sheridan County, Montana, 1918–1934." *Great Plains Quarterly,* University of Nebraska, Lincoln, 1995.

ABOUT THE AUTHOR

Jo Anne Salisbury Troxel is a third-generation Montanan who grew up on the Flathead/Salish/Kootenai reservation at Arlee, Montana. She received her undergraduate and master's degree from Montana State University. She also attended summer school for seven years at Christ Church, Oxford, England.

She retired from Headwaters Academy in Bozeman in the spring of 2003, where as head of the English Department, she organized an innovative program for the high school. Previous to that, she taught English and creative writing for twenty-three years at Bozeman Senior High School, as well as conducting writing workshops in Bozeman and around the state. She is a grassroots organizer and activist, and over the years has been involved with social issues such as women's rights, the environment, and universal health. She helped organize the local Gallatin Valley Human Rights Task Force. Most recently, she has been on the advisory board of KGVM, Gallatin Valley Community Radio. She is also active in the Unitarian Universalist Fellowship of Bozeman.

She is a passionate supporter of the arts and served on the Montana Arts Council for several years, and was also president of Beall Park Art Center, relocated now to the Emerson Cultural Center.

She is still writing.

ALSO BY
Jo Anne Salisbury Troxel

"Through a Golden Lens," published in *Bozeman From the Heart*, a collection of Bozeman writers as well as paintings by June Safford. Edited by June Safford and Paula Beswick, 2019.

Mean Dog Blues, a book of poems, 2016.

"Four Generations of Women: A Cautionary Tale." Presentation for Women's History Month at Montana State University, 2015.

"Four Generations of Women: A Cautionary Tale." Presentation for Women's History Month at Elling House, Center for Art and Culture, Virginia City, Montana, 2015.

"Movers and Shakers, the 70s." (100th Anniversary of the Suffragettes) Montana State University, 2014.

"Rodney Salisbury, Communist Sheriff of Sheridan County." Presentation for Pecha Kucha at the Ellen Theater, 2013.

"Health Care Stories." Reader's Theater, presented at Bozeman Public Library, 2012.

"Buddhist Inspired Poetry." Reader's Theater, presented at the Country Bookshelf, Bozeman, Montana, 2010.

Distinctly Montana Magazine: "The Buddha Garden at Arlee." Spring, 2010.

Poems Across the Big Sky, An Anthology of Montana Poets: "Finley Creek." 2007.